Exploring the Autobiography as a Genre and a Data Collection Tool

Exploring the Autobiography as a Genre and a Data Collection Tool

Edited by

Nadia Abid and Elena Bonta

**Cambridge
Scholars**
Publishing

Exploring the Autobiography as a Genre and a Data Collection Tool

Edited by Nadia Abid and Elena Bonta

This book first published 2023

Cambridge Scholars Publishing

Lady Stephenson Library, Newcastle upon Tyne, NE6 2PA, UK

British Library Cataloguing in Publication Data
A catalogue record for this book is available from the British Library

ISBN (10): 1-5275-3172-4
ISBN (13): 978-1-5275-3172-7

TABLE OF CONTENTS

LIST OF ILLUSTRATIONS

LIST OF TABLES

ACKNOWLEDGMENTS

This volume is the outcome of a cooperation between two groups of researchers based two universities, namely the University of Sfax, Tunisian and "Vasile Alecsandri" University of Bacău, Romania. We would like to thank the contributors for their cooperation and devotion all along the process of writing this volume. We are grateful to them for the time they gave and efforts they made to review and proofread the chapters.

The editor Nadia Abid is especially grateful to her co-editor, Prof. Elena Bonta for her valuable advice and encouragement all along the process of editing this volume despite the hard moments she went through while working on the volume.

PREFACE

MARICELA STRUNGARIU
ASSOCIATE PROFESSOR, PhD - DEPARTMENT OF FOREIGN
LANGUAGES AND LITERATURES, "VASILE ALECSANDRI"
UNIVERSITY, OF BACĂU, ROMANIA

Talking about the world means, to a certain extent, talking about oneself, transposing linguistically, in a more or less faithful way, fragments of one's own mental, spiritual or emotional universe. When the self becomes the object of our discourse, a decentring movement occurs simultaneously, an outwards flight of the, a search for otherness, because the word is always addressed to someone, its meaning being constructed, at the same time, by to the one who utters it and by the one who receives it.

The awareness of one's own self, as well as the discourse about oneself, is achieved through the words of another, because language is the product of alterity. Thus, the particular and the general intertwine, and intimacy tends towards universality. Talking about oneself presupposes a survey of the ego, of the ontological contours of one's own being, an awareness of singularity, but also of belonging to humanity, because, as Montaigne said, "...every man carries within himself the entire form of the human condition". The ego can only think in relation to the other, to alterity. Autobiographical texts reflect this duality through a perpetual oscillation between exteriority and interiority, recording the fluctuations and movements of the ego between itself and the other.

The discourse about oneself is not a verbal transposition of a well-defined and immutable intimate space, because the self is in a continuous process of construction, and this construction also takes place through discourse. Therefore, talking about yourself also means inventing yourself, building an identity. Autobiography, in its various forms, translates, first of all, this desire of the subject to know himself, to give his existence a meaning, a unity, to reveal his uniqueness, thus fighting against time, oblivion and dissolution.

In order to know himself better, however, the subject must redouble himself, distance himself from himself, objectify himself, treating himself as if he were another, an almost impossible mission for a man fascinated by his own individuality.

Whether it is literary or non-literary autobiography, linguistic autobiography or any other form of autobiographical writing, the stakes, the challenges, and the difficulties converge towards the same issue: how to get to the truth using tools specific to mystification? Autobiographical texts form a contradictory, paradoxical genre, trying to reconcile the desire for authenticity and the artifices they have to resort to in order to transpose life discursively. Sincerity and truthfulness are constantly undermined by psychological, linguistic and narrative factors that prove the fragility of any autobiographical approach. The difficulty of the subject to know himself and to express through linguistic means the richness of his inner experiences is doubled by that of reconstructing his personal history, because the process of recollection depends strictly on the functioning of memory, a memory that often proves to be laconic, unfaithful and selective.

As a palliative for the insufficiency of memory, the authors resort, quite often, to imagination or fiction, which blatantly contradicts the autobiographical pact. Hence, the tendency, registered in the last decades, to transgress generic borders, to resort to hybrid forms of writing, such as the autobiographical novel, literary self-portrait or auto-fiction.

Surprisingly, autobiography is renewed, reinvented precisely by dissolving the limits and principles that imposed it as a genre. Initially aiming to reveal the truth about oneself, the writing of the self easily slips into fabulation and fiction - provisional and limited solutions that represent, properly speaking, a failed experience of self-representation.

The few general considerations above are intended to open a field of reflections on the possibility of existence and manifestation of a genre that has been trying, for more than two centuries, to outline its principles, limits and fix its status within discursive forms.

INTRODUCTION

NADIA ABID AND ELENA BONTA

Autobiography is defined by Britannica as "the biography of oneself narrated by oneself". It is a kind of narrative that is introspective and useful for self-discovery (Clandnin and Hubet, 2010; Thurlow, 2004; Trahar, 2009), reconstruction of reality (Pavlenko and Lantoff, 2000), identity (re)construction, and self-reflection (Kilianska-Przbylo, 2012). Autobiographies can be religious, philosophical, artistic and fictionalized and take different forms including poems, novels, letters, diaries, journals and confessions. Recently, they are adopted in foreign language education where they serve as a tool for teaching and self-reflection on teaching practices and language and intercultural learning.

Autobiographies can, therefore, be considered as a genre and a tool of inquiry and data collection. In this book, seven chapters deal with autobiography both as a genre and a data collection method. The authors selected various sub-genres of autobiographies including confessional poems, autobiographical novels, politicians' narratives, commencement speeches, and teachers' and students' autobiographies and approached from different perspectives using varied analytic tools such as thematic analysis, conceptual metaphors, multi-modal analysis and appraisal theory. The multi-perspectival approach to the exploration of various types of autobiographies can be of great benefit to researchers and teachers in different disciplines in humanities as they provide insights on the different approaches to analyze autobiographies and what these approaches reveal in terms of generic features, themes, language use and implication for research and teaching.

In literature, autobiographical poems are explored to show how poets' selves are revealed in their psychological, cultural, biological and social dimensions. For instance, Elena Ciobanu's chapter, entitled "An Art lined with flesh: Autobiographical underpinnings in American confessional poetry", focused on a type of poetry which is a significant part of a cultural phenomenon that concentrates on confession as a sort of unrestrained, and quite open, communication to the other (be they a psychiatrist, a friend or a reader) of rather embarrassing personal issues.

The chapter deals with the manner in which this kind of poetic writing brings to the fore the Self, displayed with a stunning frankness and courage and who confesses things previously deemed unacceptable as literary topics, things that had only formed the matter of private conversations.

Applied linguistics has been interested in studying autobiographies. As a multidisciplinary field, Applied Linguistics has provided analytic and theoretical frameworks for the analysis of different types of discourses. In "Autobiographical metaphors in Michelle Obama's *Becoming*", Gabriela Andrioai and Alexandra Moraru attempt to reveal the deep structure concepts encoded in the life story of a famous person. Taking cognitive semantics as a starting point in their analysis, the authors focus on decoding the conceptual metaphors in Michelle Obama's autobiography, as well as the specific roles in terms of linguistic projections of cultural identities.

As a discourse that can have different forms, verbal and nonverbal, autobiographies can also lend themselves to other types of analyses relevant to the specificity and generic features of the genre. Dorra Moalla, in her chapter entitled "Autobiographical Commencement Speeches: Perspectives from Genre, Appraisal, and Multimodality", analyses commencement speeches that celebrities deliver in American universities during graduation ceremonies. The author used a combination of multimodality, appraisal theory and genre analysis to show how the self is constructed through the analysis of the speeches' generic patterns reflected at the verbal and non-verbal aspects of discourse.

In foreign language education, autobiographies have recently been adopted by teachers and students as instruments of reflection on their own experiences with language learning and intercultural encounters. Raluca Galiţa and Elena Bonta's chapter, "Critical thinking at play in language autobiographies. The case of intellectual perseverance", is based on a qualitative approach, having as research instrument a personal type of narrative account: language autobiography. The authors start from the assumption that if teachers understand, through critical reflection, the whole process through which they acquired/learned a new language – establishing their goals, overcoming obstacles and frustrations on the way to attaining their objectives – they could improve their teaching strategies, techniques and behaviours used in their teaching process.

In the context of study abroad programs and the challenges they pose for students, Nadia Abid and Asma Moalla's chapter entitled "Developing Host Communication Competence in study abroad programs. A study of Tunisian students' autobiographies of intercultural encounters" explores the processes of developing HCC that twelve Tunisian students went through while trying to adapt to the host environment. The use of the Autobiography of Intercultural Encounters (AIE) as a tool of data collection revealed the mutual influence of the different competences constituting HCC in real intercultural contacts and highlighted the transformational process that SA students went through to integrate in the host community.

While the main focus in Abid and Moalla's paper is intercultural development and transformation during study abroad programs, Sadok Damak's paper "Interculturality as the outcome of religious cultural encounters in the autobiography of Malcolm X" has tackled the issue of intercultural experience and its effect on identity reconstruction in the *Autobiography of Malcolm X.* The autobiography offers a first-hand account of Malcom X's religious experience inside the Nation of Islam, which led to his conversion from Christianity to Islam. It reports on the cultural changes brought forth by the Nation of Islam not only in the personal life of the author of this self-account but also even in the attitudes of the sect's disciples at large.

Autobiographies can be written by famous political figures to talk about their experiences while in power and when taking critical decisions. Fathi Bourmeche, in his chapter "David Cameron's account of the Brexit Referendum: What does it bring forth," attempts to shed light on the Brexit referendum held on 23 June 2016 from the point of view of David Cameron, the Prime Minister, at the tile. The study analysed Cameron's own narrative of the campaign as revealed in chapter 46 entitled "referendum" in his autobiography entitled *For the Record.* Based on a qualitative analysis, the study argues that Cameron's own version of the Brexit campaign seems to be a confession about his failure to keep his close friends' support in an atmosphere of divisions and resignations within the Conservative Party and to gain the support of the British media despite his repeated attempts to convince them to remain in the European Union. The study highlights the significance of autobiographies in unveiling realities, whether those of events depicted or of the personal lives of their main characters.

As a summary, the seven chapters attempted to explore autobiographies as genres produced in different disciplines with different communicative purposes, discourse structures and language that helped construct and reconstruct identities and perspectives. Autobiographies are also explored as data collection method that served as self-reflection on experiences in different contexts, namely those related to the teaching profession. The autobiographies selected revealed interesting insights in different human experiences characterized by contradictions, thoughts etc.

CHAPTER 1

AN ART LINED WITH FLESH: AUTOBIOGRAPHICAL UNDERPINNINGS IN AMERICAN CONFESSIONAL POETRY

ELENA CIOBANU

Introduction

Our contemporary world loves the idea of confession. It is not confession in its old religious sense, but confession as a sort of unrestrained, and quite open, communication to the other (be they a psychiatrist, a friend or a reader) of rather embarrassing personal issues. This is seen not only in the ways in which literature based on biography thrives nowadays, but also in the complex development of some significant artistic trends and paradigms in the latter decades. The type of poetry this chapter focuses on is a significant part of such a cultural phenomenon, as it purports, in stark opposition to Modernist injunctions, to tell the truth, as it were.

The cultural landscape was quite different when Robert Lowell published his *Life Studies* (1959), a volume considered by many scholars as nothing less than a revolutionary moment in the history of Anglo-American poetry. At that time, the Western literary scene had been dominated for almost half a century by T. S. Eliot's dictum saying that "poetry is not a turning loose of emotion, but an escape from emotion; it is not the expression of personality, but an escape from personality" (Eliot 1920: 53). Eliot was still alive when M. L. Rosenthal's review of Lowell's book definitively associated the term 'confessional' with a type of poetic discourse that would have been anathema for Eliot and whose main, and almost exclusive, topic was the self and its tribulations. Nonetheless, the adjective turned out to be "both helpful and too limited" for Rosenthal, who later wondered whether "the conception of a confessional school" had not "done a certain amount of damage" (1967: 23).

For one thing, the confessional mode was not a completely new invention. It stemmed from a tradition that included great figures like Rilke, Baudelaire or Whitman. The great Walt was actually acknowledged as a precursor by some of the Confessional poets (John Berryman and Theodore Roethke, among others). One may even say that "if Robert Lowell is the father" of the Confessional group, "Whitman is the great-grandfather" (Phillips 1973: 3). Thus, the confessional mode "has always been with us" (*ibidem*), even though it was given an 'official' name rather recently at the scale of human history.

Written in opposition to the impersonal aesthetic dictated by Eliot, this kind of poetic writing brings to the fore the Self, displayed with a stunning frankness and courage. The absolute newness of this poetry constitutes in the fact that it 'confessed' things previously deemed unacceptable as literary topics, things that had only formed the matter of private conversations. Confessional poets "describe aspects of their lives that most people would conceal, such as impulses to suicide, abject humiliations and lusts, and hatred of their families" (Perkins 1987: 343). Rather than avoiding emotion, as Modernist predecessors taught, poets like Robert Lowell, John Berryman, Sylvia Plath or Anne Sexton turned emotion into the main concern of their discourse, marked as it is by the presence of afflicted protagonists who are doomed to ask unanswerable questions in a futile search for liberation and detachment.

In the work of these poets, autobiography is an essential element, not only as the matter that is endlessly probed and exploited, but also as a source of an unusual kind of semantic and structural coherence. Robert Lowell once declared that the thread keeping his art together through the years was precisely his autobiography. His poems are structures of experience mediating between himself and his world, between "his personal history and that of his readers" (Axelrod 1978: 4). Lowell's excruciating artistic task seems to have been the finding of the appropriate metaphorical forms for the expression and elucidation of the meanings of his biographical issues. Art and life, in Lowell's thought, entertained a complex interrelationship: "his life made his writing possible, and the ability to write saved his life and gave it meaning" (Axelrod 1978: 6). Art is in fact the result of the working up of experience into form, and this, in turn, bestows meaning on the life out of which that experience was extracted. It appears that "Autobiography, with its basically stable theory of causation, its firm checks upon reality and dream, its ordered sense of past, present, and future, was for him a necessary condition for continued survival" (Chiasson 2017). In a similar manner, Sylvia Plath repeatedly declared in her journal that "the colossal job of merely living" (Plath 2000:

184) could never be enough for her. Her true existence depended on how well she would manage to satisfy her "urge to excel in one medium of translation and expression of life". She desperately confessed to herself: "I can't be satisfied with the colossal job of merely living. Oh, no, I must order life in sonnets and sestinas and provide a verbal reflector for my 60-watt lighted head" (Plath 2000: 184). Plath achieves her poetic masterpieces only after numerous painful attempts to create "a rich and meaningful pattern" (Plath 2000: 342) able to express and contain the "one vulnerable spot in the hard, frozen, acrid little core" (Plath 2000: 152) in herself. Her diaries abundantly offer proofs of her anxious complaining about her inability to use "all the wasteful accident of life" (Plath 2000: 342) in order "to articulate the vague seething desires" (Plath 2000: 151) in her.

1. Unhealable wounds

The energy fuelling such desires to turn life into words on a page seems to have been intimately linked with the psychological issues that tormented these poets throughout their lives. Coincidentally or not, most of those belonging to the Confessional school suffered from mental illnesses that often led them to episodes of intense suffering and, eventually, suicide.[1] Diagnosed as manic-depressive, most of these poets were prone to unimaginable depths of pain that often turned them into patients of psychiatric hospitals in the wake of more or less successful suicide attempts.

Robert Lowell spent his life in and out of such institutions, and, in the periods of relative sanity, his relations with his family were dramatically affected by the consequences of the recurring crises he could not really contain: "When he was manic, Lowell smashed wineglasses and schemed to marry near-strangers. In recovery, his depressions were severe, his remorse profound, the work of repairing the relationships he'd damaged unrelenting. But the metaphors that came so quickly to hand could again be tamed and put to use." (Chiasson 2017). His verse openly approaches such issues, with sincerity and self-irony. In *Home After Three Months Away*, the poetic voice touchingly addresses his relationship with his infant daughter whose reassuring joy at his coming home makes him feel regret and responsibility:

---

[1] To give just a few examples, Sylvia Plath gassed herself in 1963 in her London flat, while her two children were sleeping in the next room; John Berryman threw himself off Minneapolis bridge in 1972; Anne Sexton committed suicide in 1974.

"Three months, three months!
Is Richard now himself again?
Dimpled with exaltation,
my daughter holds her levee in the tub.
Our noses rub,
each of us pats a stringy lock of hair –
they tell me nothing's gone.
Though I am forty-one,
not forty now, the time I put away
was child's play." (Lowell 2001: 16)

The tenderness that permeates the description of the child is paralleled by an equivocal recovery whose end is not very promising for the speaker: "Recuperating, I neither spin, nor toil" (Lowell 2001: 17). The image of "our coffin's length of soil", where "seven horizontal tulips blow", undistinguishable from weed, unable to "meet another year's snowballing enervation" (Lowell 2001: 16), suggests something incongruous with the paradigm of healing. The return to normality brings no exhilaration or satisfaction: "I keep no rank nor station. / Cured, I am frizzled, stale and small" (Lowell 2001: 17).

Other poems even suggest that this return to normality is more of an illusion. The descriptions of the figures from "the house for 'the mentally ill'" in *Waking in the Blue* are marked by the perception of a psychic immobility out of which it is hard to imagine them. Former glory and "kingly" attributes are in stark contrast to a desolating present where "Stanley", "once a Harvard all-American fullback", "now sunk in his sixties", does nothing but soak "in his long tub, / vaguely ruinous from the Victorian plumbing" and "thinks only of his figure, / of slimming on sherbet and ginger ale". Similarly, "Bobbie, / Porcellian '29", despite his physical resemblance to Louis XVI, is "redolent and roly-poly as a sperm whale, / as he swashbuckles about in his birthday suit / and horses at chairs" (Lowell 2001: 14). The way out of such "ossified" conditions is ultimately impossible for the speaker of the poem, who identifies with his fellow patients and their irreversible fates: "We are all old-timers, / each of us holds a locked razor" (Lowell 2001: 15). Such poems do but confirm the professional conclusion of an acclaimed psychiatrist like Kay Redfield Jamison, for whom it is clear that "Robert Lowell had a severe form of manic-depressive illness. When mania came, it was brutal; when it left there remained depression, remorse and the certainty it would be back" (Jamison 2017: 254). Yet Jamison also notices the admirable courage with which Lowell dealt with the pain and fear inextricably linked with his illness.

No less courageously did other confessional poets approach the theme of ineffectual medical treatment and ambiguous recuperation on return from hospital. In *Tulips*, Plath's disappointed tone points towards an elusive state of health that is highly questionable. The "too excitable" redness of the tulips "hurts" and "talks" to the persona's "wounds", dragging her from her pure death-like "peacefulness" where everything is white, quiet and "snowed-in" (Plath 1981: 160). The process of healing is metaphorically rendered as an aggression: the smiles of the loved ones whose photos the patient sees on her night table are hooks catching unto her skin, the tulips are "a dozen red lead sinkers round my neck", "a loud voice" or "dangerous animals" (Plath 1981: 162). Rather unwillingly, the persona finishes by tasting water that is "warm and salt, like the sea, / And comes from a country as far away as health" (Plath 1981: 162). In *Poem for a Birthday*, the same process of recovery is ironically encapsulated in the image of the "reconstructed" vase that "houses / The elusive rose" (Plath 1981: 137). There simply is no real possibility for the Plathian self to fully regain her sense of plenitude and balance. Even in the poems where her avatars declare their victories over the dark forces that keep them captive, the triumphs feel always unsure and only temporary. In *Stings*, for example, the queen-bee that is flying "more terrible than she ever was, red / Scar in the sky, red comet / Over the engine that killed her - / The mausoleum, the wax house" has "wings of glass" (Plath 1981: 215): they can hardly guarantee a safe flight towards freedom.

Psychiatric treatment, despite its eventual inefficiency, seems to have played a positive, if provisional, role in the life of Anne Sexton. When she began writing poems, it was due to her psychiatrist's advice during the many sessions of treatment of her postpartum depression after she gave birth to her first child in 1953. Dr. Martin Orne took over her case from his mother, who had treated Sexton previously, and turned into a sort of Pygmalion figure for the poet, the latter even claiming that he had co-created her poetic identity, as it was under his guidance that she could channel her energies towards manifesting her creativity in writing. The therapy tapes that are now controversially public demonstrate that her artistic output was indeed one of the effects of Dr. Martin Orne's telling her that "her diagnostic tests revealed that she was very creative" (Skorczewski 2012: xvi) and that she could use what she envisaged as her sexual power in writing about her experiences.

The volume *To Bedlam and Part Way Back*, published in the same year (1960) as Plath's *The Colossus and Other Poems*, contains poems where dialogues between doctor and patient are staged that show us the process of self-empowerment leading the feminine voice from sins and conventional beauty to authentic identity. "You, Doctor Martin", begins the persona in the first poem from Sexton's volume, "walk from breakfast to madness", while she is "queen of this summer hotel / or the laughing bee on a stalk" (Sexton 1988: 9). At the end, her self emerges as much better defined:

> "I am queen of all my sins
> Forgotten. Am I still lost?
> Once I was beautiful. Now I am myself,
> Counting this row and that row of moccasins
> Waiting on the silent shelf." (Sexton 1988: 10)

2. The Oedipal nexus

The roots of such mental illnesses are often profoundly intertwined with family problems that are brought to the surface in such confessional poems in sometimes shocking ways. Most frequently, the main interest is in "the family interpreted in a Freudian perspective: the family is a nexus of rivalry and emotional ambivalence; parents and children view each other through distorting psychological projections" (Perkins 1987: 343). Deliberately adopting psychoanalytical concepts and paradigms, the poets of this school weave them in their texts in order to painfully explore and hopefully escape their inscrutable suffering. Damaged relationships between depressed sons/daughters and castrating or painfully indifferent fathers/mothers, between cruel husbands and discontent wives find disturbing literary expressions.

The tensions in the Lowell household while Robert was a child made him experience alternating bouts of rage and gloom, and his confessional poems make no secret of his mother's domineering nature or of his father's ineffectual presence. In *Commander Lowell*, the poetic voice bitterly remembers how

> "There were no undesirables or girls in my set,
> When I was a boy at Mattapoiset –
> Only Mother, still her Father's daughter.
> Her voice was still electric
> With a hysterical, unmarried panic,
> When she read to me from the Napoleon book." (Lowell 1977: 76)

His mother's dissatisfaction with her husband is echoed in the child's shame at his father's eccentric appearance in places where he is obviously not at ease at all: "He wasn't at all 'serious,' / when he showed up on the golf course, / wearing a blue serge jacket and numbly cut / white ducks he'd bought / at a Pearl Harbour commissariat..." (Lowell 1977: 76). At first having been a naval officer, Commander Lowell turns out to be incapable of managing his professional life and successively loses various jobs, thus rendering his family financially vulnerable. His son sadly narrates the degradation of his life, which appears all the more regrettable when compared to his initial success. Yet, it is impossible now to find a stable paternal presence in this "poor Father" who was once "successful enough to be lost / in the mob of ruling-class Bostonians" (Lowell 1977: 78). Not even by going backwards in memory as far as the period when the father, "the youngest ensign in his class, [...] was 'the old man' of a gun boat on the Yangtze" (Lowell 1977: 78) can the son recover a sense of dependable fatherhood.

Combining autobiography and myth, Sylvia Plath's image of the father is far more menacing than Lowell's. True to her desire of extrapolating her experiences, Plath remoulds the figure of Otto (her father who died when she was eight and thus left her traumatized for life) into that of an inscrutable and dictatorial father whose words, gestures, appearances and deeds keep the daughter-persona forever prisoner. In Plath's earlier poetry, the daughter resignedly accepts that the longed-for patriarch is unreachable and irretrievable. *Full Fathom Five* revolves around this theme as it contemplates "the old myth of origins / Unimaginable", that is, the "old man" with many dangers who reappears despite rumours of having been buried, all-powerful and defying, just like a god. The daughter is "Exiled to no good" while she is walking on his kingdom's border in a "thick" and "murderous" (Plath 1981: 92-93) air. The metaphor of the colossus from another poem maintains the supremacy of the paternal image whose "Mule-bray, pig-grunt and bawdy cackles" (Plath 1981: 128) remain incomprehensible and oppressive to the girl uselessly toiling to reconstruct him. His "dark funnel" (Plath 1981: 187) of language from *Little Fugue* still ensnares her years later, even in the poems of apparent rebellion and transcendence. In the famous *Daddy* poem, paternal discourse is figured as "a barb wire snare", as a "gobbledygoo" (Plath 1981: 222) that continues to wreak havoc on her. The daughter's heroic attempts to liberate herself from the "panzer-man", the "Fascist" (Plath 1981: 223), vampire, devil father, are eventually tinged with a dismaying ambiguity:

"There's a stake in your fat black heart
And the villagers never liked you.
They are dancing and stamping on you.
They always knew it was you.
Daddy, daddy, you bastard, I'm through." (Plath 1981: 224)

The Plathian avatars are equally unable to liberate themselves from the suffocating domination of the mother-figure, metaphorically referred to as an unwanted medusa that feeds on her "overexposed" (Plath 1981: 225) daughter. In *Medusa*, the maternal "eely tentacle" superposed on religious images of a "Ghastly Vatican" paralyses "the kicking lovers" while it is "touching and sucking" (Plath 1981: 225-226) the very life out of her vulnerable daughter. Imagining herself as a sort of Electra (Plath 1981: 116), the persona is forever marked by her mother's 'murder' of her father, and by the mother's inability to defend her children against the deadly presence of the mysterious "disquieting muses" (Plath 1981: 74) nodding their heads over their cribs.

Anne Sexton's poetic persona nurtures the same type of perturbed relationship with her conventional and cold mother. In *The Double Image*, this mother "cannot forgive" (Sexton 1999: 35) the daughter's suicide, which she takes as a personal offense. She does her best though, as she takes her daughter to the hairdresser's and orders her portrait to be done, ignoring that meanwhile the same daughter whom she treats like an insensitive doll feels "like an angry guest, / like a partly mended thing, an outgrown child" (Sexton 1999: 42). In *The Division of Parts*, the persona openly curses the indifferent mother in a "jabbering dream":

> "I heard my own angry cries
> and I cursed you, Dame
> keep out of my slumber.
> My good Dame, you are dead.
> And Mother, three stones
> slipped from your glittering eyes." (Sexton 1999: 45)

The disappointment inherent in marriage relations echoes and continues those of the primordial family knot in the work of confessional poets. Robert Lowell's *Man and Wife* depicts a couple doomed by a series of problems. The perceptions of the male voice observing the room where the two spouses lie "on Mother's bed" are marked by an insidious violence seen in the "war paint" of the "rising sun" or in the ways in which "our magnolia ignite / the morning with their murderous five days' white" (Lowell 2001: 20). The chilling lack of communication from the last stanza completely erases the last memory traces of a past tenderness, itself subverted by shyness or by defiant attitudes:

> "Now twelve years later, you turn your back.
> Sleepless, you hold
> Your pillow to your hollows like a child;

Your old-fashioned tirade –
Loving, rapid, merciless –
Breaks like the Atlantic Ocean on my head." (Lowell 2001: 20)

In a poem with an identical title as that of Lowell's, Anne Sexton's feminine voice is even more drastic in her statement of the solitude involved in marriage: "We are not lovers. / We do not even know each other. / We look alike / but we have nothing to say. / We are like pigeons…" (Sexton 1999: 116). Lowell could also sympathize with a feminine perspective in a poem that comments on a famous medieval phrase (*'To speak of woe that is in marriage'*). [2] Here, the abused wife tries to survive in a relationship where she is a completely powerless victim: "My only thought is how to keep alive. / What makes him tick? Each night now I tie / ten dollars and his car key to my thigh" (Lowell 2001: 21).

Sylvia Plath's poems on this topic bring forth images of marital relations that are even more extreme in their implied violence and cruelty. In opposition to the admiration and love for one's spouse that are manifest in some earlier texts, the Plathian husband personae in her later work can be merciless rabbit catchers, zoo-keepers, jailors or beekeepers who can only possess, subdue, torture and eventually kill their wife-prisoners. The figure of the husband is also superposed on that of the evil father, as in *Daddy*, where the daughter-persona has to kill both the Nazi father and "the vampire who said he was you / And drank my blood for a year, / Seven years, if you want to know" (Plath 1981: 223).

Inescapably caught in such failed relationships, the speakers of confessional poems have to endure an existence that does not allow them to perform acts of authentic liberation from their inner demons. Thus, their selves remain fragile, incompletely defined, always more or less dependent on a menacing otherness that they have to fight if they want to circumscribe a space of their own.

3. Sincerity as convention

The danger always lurking in such writing is that it may lose its relevance to others, oblivious as they may be of the personal allusions and meanings contained in the text. This is why the hardest task of the confessional poets was to open up their experience in an effort to enable their readers to fathom their idiosyncrasies. In a 1966 interview with Peter Orr, Sylvia Plath declared her admiration for the confessional mode, for its "intense

---

[2] This phrase is used by Chaucer's famous Wife of Bath from his *Canterbury Tales* (Chaucer 1951: 310).

breakthrough into very serious, very personal, emotional experience which I feel has been partly taboo". At the same time, she was aware that personal experiences should be "manipulated" "with an informed and intelligent mind" in order for them to be rendered "relevant to the larger things such as Hiroshima and Dachau and so on" (Plath 1966).

Success in such a manipulation of personal matter may be seen in how some critics have rightfully argued that confessional poetry derives its value not from biographical details but from the artistic strategies by means of which life is turned into art. After all, poetic meaning must be the successful outcome of a complex synthesis between experience and language. Educated in universities at a time when the New Critical dogma was dominant, the confessional poets brought into their writing the poetic principles and technical knowledge that had been so dear to I. A. Richards or T. S. Eliot. They passed from initial stages during which they tried to write poetry in the previous modes to mature phases where they managed to find their artistic voices and selves. Courageously undertaking to represent the Self as it had never been represented before, in all its splendour and, more conspicuously, in all its miseries, Lowell, Snodgrass, Roethke, Plath, Sexton or Berryman had to face the enormous task of dealing with the "general mess of imprecision of feeling, / Undisciplined squads of emotion" (Eliot 2002: 190) that anguished T. S. Eliot so much.

Their revolutionary work, while it contested the modes of the past, knew how to mould the forms of that past for present purposes. A vast familiarity with the previous literary and cultural canon helped such writers to find echoes, correspondences and partial illuminations of their topics not only in mythology but also in more contemporary paradigms like psychoanalysis. Therefore, poetic confession emerges as just another literary convention. It has elements of fancy, like any other piece of literature, and it avoids telling only the literal truth that, in itself, has no artistic relevance. Confessional poems often contain falsifications or distortions of reality for the sake of developing a certain theme or image. This is why biographical approaches to such poetry may lead to pernicious results. Their sincerity must be taken with a grain of salt, otherwise we might believe that Anne Sexton had a brother killed in the war (which she hadn't), or that Sylvia Plath's father had been a Nazi officer (which he hadn't).

Biographers and critics alike may often fall into the trap of such an approach which reduces poetry to its sources or which uses poems as witnesses in trials meant to decide where the truth resides or to identify the culprit. Sylvia Plath's case is illustrative in this respect. For a long time, the Plath scholarship used to be divided into two camps that were either on

Plath's or on Hughes' side. The fierce debate was somewhat appeased by Hughes' death in 1998, a few months after he had published *Birthday Letters*, a volume of poems entirely dedicated to the memory of his life together with Plath. Fortunately, the criticism of latter decades has cultivated much more constructive perspectives that emphasize the positive parts of the two poets' former relationship and marriage by focusing on their art rather than on the life it used to feed upon.

Confessional poets themselves took pains indeed to warn their readers that imagination was as much involved in their writing as their emotional and personal issues. In interviews and essays, they told their audiences that truth needed to be distinguished from verisimilitude when it came to their personae and images. Theodore Roethke insisted that the afflicted hero of his longer poems was a fictitious character: "Not 'I' personally, but all haunted and harried men" (Phillips 1973: 12). John Berryman denied that the Henry of his *Dream Songs* was in any consistent way to be colluded with himself: "The poem then, whatever its cast of character, is essentially about an imaginary character (not the poet, not me) named Henry" (Berryman 1968: ix). Lowell ensured his readers that his poetry was not his diary, not his "Confession, not a puritan's too literary pornographic honesty, glad to share private embarrassment and triumph" (Lowell 1969: 159). Likewise, Sylvia Plath elaborated on the larger significations associated with her personae. In a reading prepared for BBC radio, this is how she summarized the structure of her trademark *Daddy*:

> "Here is a poem spoken by a girl with an Electra complex. Her father died while she thought he was God. Her case is complicated by the fact that her father was also a Nazi and her mother very possibly part Jewish. In the daughter the two strains marry and paralyse each other – she has to act out the awful little allegory once over before she is free of it" (Plath 1981: 293).

4. The legacy of poetic confession

Such disclaimers are nevertheless relativized by the undeniable correspondences between the confessional poets' real life experience and art. Trauma, mental illness, family dysfunctions, psychiatric treatment and suicide attempts are not only artistic themes but also the matter of these lives. One cannot ignore this in the process of reading, especially in those cases where the discourse becomes highly idiosyncratic. A certain familiarity with the facts of the writer's life is required when private details are inserted in texts without any definite suggestion as to their meaning and role. Some even believe that a number of semantic obscurities cannot be deciphered unless one does it by appeal to biographical knowledge.

In his book on Plath, Hayman claims, for instance, that many of Plath's poems "contain lines which are partially or wholly incomprehensible without biographical explanation" (Hayman 1992: xviii). Among such examples we may count the image of the black telephone that is "off at the root" (Plath 1981: 224) from *Daddy* or the complaint in *The Fearful* about a woman on the telephone who pretends to be a man. Would such passages be better understood by the reader if they knew how the telephone had come to be off the root in reality or why a woman pretended to be a man while talking to Plath on the phone? Such knowledge would surely fill in the blanks left by the poet in her text that are only too difficult to reconstruct. More importantly, though, such knowledge, together with the personal issues woven in the text, contributes to the creation of a necessary verisimilitude that is an essential strategy in this kind of poetry.

Tormented to the end, confessional poets find in their art the only space where they can access meaning and psychological relief, no matter how temporary. Despite the rational element that certainly subtends confessional poetry, we must admit that this group of poets "took the blows of their mental troughs and highs to places beyond reason" (Hayes 2013: 36). This may be due, as it has been previously mentioned, to the fact that almost all of them were affected by bipolarity, a mental illness whose violent cyclicity predisposed them to unbearable alternating states of depression and wild restlessness. Psychiatric research has shown that bipolarity is intimately connected to creativity, even though a clear causal relation cannot be established between them (Jamison 1993: 48). Sometimes writers themselves confirm it: "No one has ever written, painted, sculpted, modelled, built, or invented except literally to get out of hell" (Artaud 1988: 497), Antonin Artaud wrote. And, indeed, American confessional poets, like many other writers before and after them, found in art the only escape from their psychological nightmare. For Lowell, time would not pass at all without the salutary presence of words that constitute "a sort of immense bandage of grace and ambergris for my hurt nerves" (Lowell 1990: 362). "Poetry led me by the hand out of madness" (Middlebrook 1991: 309), Anne Sexton frankly admitted. Sylvia Plath was similarly overwhelmed with joy and a respite of her suffering when she could find her way into her best poetry.

That respite has not only personal relevance, but, most importantly, it leads writers to insights with universal value. When possessed by their demanding muses, these poets become channels through which significant revelations become accessible and valuable even to those who are not challenged psychologically. It seems that

> "...familiarity with sadness and the pain of melancholy – as well as with the ecstatic, often violent energies of the manic states – can add a singular truth and power to artistic expression. To the extent that an artist survives, describes, and then transforms psychological pain into an experience with more universal meaning, his or her own journey becomes one that others can, thus better protected, take." (Jamison 1993: 120)

The creative process weaves conscious and unconscious levels in its arriving at revelatory states filling the poet's mind with the joy of what is perceived as a victory, however small, over the forces of darkness awaiting in the recesses of the mind. Fascinated by this source of personal soothing and writerly satisfaction, Sylvia Plath confesses to her journal: "My absolute lack of judgment when I've written something: whether it's trash or genius" (Plath 2000: 380). At another moment, she acknowledges the autonomy of the creative mind that follows its own inscrutable paths in the construction of its original worlds. The yew tree she once chose to put in a poem ended by taking complete possession of her consciousness:

> "...that yew tree began, with astounding egotism, to manage and order the whole affair [...] It stood squarely in the middle of my poem, manipulating its dark shades, the voices in the churchyard, the clouds, the birds, the tender melancholy with which I contemplated it." (Plath 1981: 292)

Yet the exploration of the unconscious is not only linked with what naturally inheres in human creativity. Confessional poets look deep into themselves because they are primarily interested in understanding the source of their psychic wounds. To the extent to which, by doing this, it reflects, enlightens, relieves and gives meaning to the struggles of so many others, confessional poetry acquires a value that goes beyond art, and it does so only if it convinces its readers that what it tells them is genuine. The principle, Axelrod argues, "is always the same, the growth of consciousness and the deepened sense of personal identity resulting from immersion in firsthand experience" (Axelrod 1978: 9). The illusion of absolute sincerity is thus necessary in this respect. It remains, nonetheless, an illusion.

Paradoxically, this 'sincerity' depends on an interplay of reality and fiction, a combination of real biographical details and imaginary constructs. This is the realm where Robert Lowell lived: "where deed meets word, or in his own terms, where 'what really happened' connects with the 'good line'" (Axelrod 1978: 8). We might even say that poetic confession is believed only to the measure to which that confession ceases to be only confession and becomes something more: a literary text thriving on the border between life, imagination and language. Autobiography becomes a trope in this endeavour. At this point, it no longer matters whether poetry saved or didn't save these poets from their private hells. What matters is that they managed to plunge into the impenetrable gloom of their psyche and to bring back from there visions of a strange, but very rich and empowering beauty.

References

Artaud, Antonin. 1988. "Van Gogh, the Man suicided by Society". In Antonin Artaud: Selected Writings, edited by Susan Sontag, 483-512; Berkeley and Los Angeles: University of California Press. 483-512

Axelrod, Steven. Gould. 1978. Robert Lowell. Life and Art. Princeton: Princeton University Press.

Berryman, John. 1968. His Toy, His Dream, His Rest. New York: Farrar, Straus & Giroux.

Chaucer, Geoffrey. 1951. The Canterbury Tales. London: Penguin Classics.

Chiasson, D. 2017. "The Illness and Insight of Robert Lowell". In The New Yorker, March 13th, at https://www.newyorker.com/magazine/2017/03/20/the-illness-and-insight-of-robert-lowell, retrieved 15th April 2022.

Eliot, Thomas. Stearns. 1920. The sacred wood. Essays on poetry and criticism. London: Methuen.

Eliot, Thomas. Stearns. 2002. Collected poems. London: Faber and Faber.

Hayes, Paula. 2013. Robert Lowell and the Confessional Voice. New York: Peter Lang.

Hayman, Ronald. 1992. The Death and Life of Sylvia Plath. London: Minerva.

Jamison, Kay. Redfield. 1993. Touched with Fire: Manic Depressive Illness and the Artistic Temperament. New York: Macmillan.

Jamison, Kay. Redfield. 2017. Robert Lowell: Setting the River on Fire. A Study of Genius, Mania and Character. New York: Alfred A. Knopf.

Kumin, M. 1999. "How It Was". In The Complete Poems, edited by Anne Sexton. Boston & New York: Houghton Mifflin, pp. xix-xxxiv.

Lowell, Robert. 1969. Notebook. New York: Farrar, Straus and Giroux.

Lowell, Robert. 1977. Selected Poems. New York: Farrar, Straus and Giroux.

Lowell, Robert. 1990. Collected Prose. New York: Farrar, Straus and Giroux.

Lowell, Robert. 2001. Poems selected by Michael Hoffmann. London: Faber and Faber.

Middlebrook, Diane. W. 1991. Anne Sexton: A Biography. New York: Vintage Books.

Orr, Peter. 1966. Interview with Sylvia Plath. In *The Poet Speaks: Interviews with Contemporary Poets Conducted by Hilary Morrish, Peter Orr, John Press, and Ian Scott-Kilvery.* London: Routledge, at https://www.modernamericanpoetry.org/content/1962-sylvia-plath-interview-peter-orr.

Perkins, David. 1987. A History of Modern Poetry. Modernism and After. Cambridge, Massachusetts: Belknap.

Phillips, Robert. 1973. The Confessional Poets. London: Feffer & Simons.

Plath, Sylvia. 1981. Collected Poems. Ted Hughes, ed. London: Faber and Faber.

Plath, Sylvia. 2000. The Journals of Sylvia Plath. Karen V. Kukil, ed. London: Faber and Faber.

Sexton, Anne. 1999. The Complete Poems. Boston & New York: Houghton Mifflin.

Skorczewski, Dawn. M. 2012. An Accident of Hope. The Therapy Tapes of Anne Sexton. New York: Routledge.

CHAPTER 2

AUTOBIOGRAPHICAL METAPHORS IN MICHELLE OBAMA'S *BECOMING*

GABRIELA ANDRIOAI & ALEXANDRA MORARU

Introduction

Finding its place among the series of semantic and stylistic discourse analyses, which apply linguistic and cultural theories on autobiographical texts, the present research attempts to reveal the deep structure concepts encoded in the true life story of a famous person. According to Cognitive linguistics, language use reflects inherently metaphorical understanding of many areas of experience and thus, metaphor plays an organizing factor in language and cognition (Johnson 1987; Lakoff 1987; Lakoff and Johnson 1980). That is why, metaphor exceeds being just a figure of speech and it becomes a specific mental mapping which influences the way people think, reason, and imagine in everyday life (Johnson 1987, 1993, Lakoff and Johnson 1980, Lakoff and Turner 1989). By applying the Conceptual Metaphor Theory (CMT) developed by George Lakoff and Mark Johnson in 1980, we aim at decoding the metaphors which reside at the linguistic level and depict the biographical encryption in the concepts used throughout the personal story in the book.

Michelle Obama's written account of her personal life is seen as a metaphor starting with the title itself, which encodes semantic markers of *passage*, *change*, *evolution* and *transformation*. Given the fact that the cultural representations of conceptual metaphors have an indispensable cognitive function, we shall focus on decoding the conceptual metaphors of an autobiographic nature in Michelle Obama's narrated life story, as well as specific roles in terms of linguistic projections of cultural identities.

The narrator explores the metaphorical resonance of reality and portrays herself in various different cultural, social, or personal agent-roles.

The novelty of this analysis resides in the use of the latest linguistic trend – cognitive semantics – as its most important apparatus; as well as in the application of the Conceptual Metaphor Theory by following the theoretical cognitive-semantic studies of George Lakoff (1987, 1990, 1993), Mark Johnson (1987), Lakoff and Johnson (1980), Lakoff and Turner (1989), Gilles Fauconnier (2002), Gibbs (2011), Kövecses (2017) and others.

Theoretical Background

The principles of cognitive semantics and conceptual metaphor theory successfully blend together with the theory of autobiography. Therefore, even if it is notoriously difficult to define autobiography, in the broader sense of the word it is used almost synonymously with "self-representation" and denotes all modes and genres of telling one's own life story. More specifically, autobiography as a literary genre signifies a retrospective narrative that undertakes to tell the author's own life, or a substantial part of it, seeking (at least in its classic version) to reconstruct his/her personal development within a given historical, social and cultural framework. Autobiographers set forth a view of what is called the inner Self and its doings, reflections, thoughts, and place in the world (Gilmore 1994). By no means, an autobiography depicts the most important challenges and events in the author's life whose purpose is to educate the readers and to make them understand the lives of others who come from different backgrounds. In addition, through an autobiography, readers may examine how different cultural elements shaped their identity. For Michelle Obama, *Becoming "is a powerful sense of self"* and, as she explains in the Epilogue, by writing her autobiography, she was just trying to share her story in her own way. No matter the reason for which autobiographers write their stories, readers may increase their understanding by learning from other people's experiences, reflect on their personal beliefs and even shape their own identities guided or motivated by famous people.

The core theoretical structure of this research represents a projection mapping which outlines structure from one domain (source) onto another (target). In fact, metaphors function as maps, which guide us from a concrete source domain to an abstract target domain at a conceptual level. Thus, the target domain is understood by the logic of the source domain, highlighting the different aspects of the target domain. Pragmatic function mappings occur between two entities based on a shared frame of experience. For example, metonymy, which depends upon an association between two entities so that one entity can stand for the other, is an instance of a pragmatic function mapping. Schema mappings relate to the projection of a schema (another term for frame) onto particular utterances. Cognitive semanticists treat meaning construction as a process that is fundamentally conceptual in nature. From this perspective, sentences work as "partial instructions" for the construction of complex but temporary conceptual domains assembled as a result of ongoing discourse. These domains, which are called mental spaces, are linked to one another in various ways, allowing speakers to "link back" to mental spaces constructed earlier in the ongoing linguistic exchange. From this perspective, meaning is not a property of individual sentences, nor simply a matter of their interpretation relative to the external world. Instead, meaning arises from a dynamic process of meaning construction, which we call conceptualisation.

Nevertheless, as Vyvyan Evans and Melanie Green (2006: 153) have summed up, the guiding principles of cognitive semantics are as follows: conceptual structure is embodied, semantic structure is conceptual structure, meaning representation is encyclopaedic, meaning construction is conceptualisation. The first principle marched on one idea that has emerged in order to explain the nature of conceptual organisation based on interaction with the physical world and it is called the embodied cognition thesis.

The second principle claims that language refers to concepts in the mind of the speaker rather than to objects in the outer world. These conventional meanings associated with words are linguistic concepts or lexical concepts. They represent the conventional form that is required by conceptual structure to be encoded in language. However, the claim that semantic structure can be equated with conceptual structure does not mean that the two are identical. On the contrary, cognitive semanticists assert that words and meanings together form only a subset of possible concepts. The other concepts, which do not have a correspondent word associated with meaning, stand proof for the fact that thought precedes language.

Conceptual Metaphor Analysis

Psychoanalysis and cultural studies are of great importance when studying the cultural identities and representations of Michelle Obama's evolution because they combine communication with sociology, social theory, literary theory, philosophy and cultural anthropology. Therefore, the main source domains of our conceptual metaphors revolve around the ideas of family, politics and personal development, and the way they interconnect throughout the text. Michelle Obama portrays herself as a daughter, an adult/young woman at the beginning of her career, wife, mother, professional and First Lady, which all converge into her "becoming" exactly as a "blooming flower". All these transformations framed by words and images have nothing to do with growing old, they are in fact the metamorphoses which stand as metaphors for change and they are central to the book.

The study is structured on three directions of analysis that correspond to the three parts of the novel and which incorporate the journey of becoming – Becoming Me – the change in the process of becoming – Becoming Us – and the voice of becoming – Becoming More. Following this concept of continuous evolution, we can analyse the book in terms of the conceptual metaphor LIFE IS JOURNEY, which is projected all along the life story of the former First Lady. A journey is a frequent mental association for life, as it reminds us that from a linear perspective, we always have a starting point and a destination. From a first glance, we can observe a central conceptual metaphor BECOMING IS CONTINUOUS, which is part of the same semantic sphere of the corollary one – LIFE IS A JOURNEY. Close attention needs also to be paid to the phenomenon of metaphoric amalgams, which arise from the principled integration of two metaphors into one single conceptual construct. Thus, the two metaphors combine the mental constructs of transformation, process, continuum, and other lexical items of the semantic sphere of *becoming* but the basic layout are the core conceptual metaphor LIFE IS A JOURNEY.

The first conceptual metaphor that is related to the field of autobiography is BECOMING IS CONTINUOUS. Becoming is part of the self-understanding process and it opens up a new path towards a new life story. It is a continuous development which may take a life-time. This conceptualization of lifelong learning and constant evolution is projected from the beginning of the book in all its three parts, which are simply but so effectively entitled: *Becoming Me, Becoming Us* and *Becoming More*. The whole book proves Michelle Obama's powerful sense of self, emphasizing all the important stages in her life together with the roles that she had skilfully accomplished. The metaphor BECOMING IS CONTINUOUS projects the image of a soul with an immensity of emotions and of an optimist spirit with large visions who dares to declare confidently:

> *"Now I think it's one of the most useless questions an adult can ask a child —What do you want to be when you grow up? **As if growing up is finite**. As if at some point you become something and that's the end."* (16)

Although the author uses the opposite idea "growing up is finite", she chooses to employ the conditional "as if" which refers to something that the speaker deems very unlikely, therefore changing the meaning and reversing the semantic markers to [+CONTINUITY, +FLOW, +CONTINUUM]. The process of growing contains an inner, deeper meaning that suggests a type of movement that can be accomplished both on the horizontal axis, as well as on the vertical. It is up to each of us to overcome the obstacles along the journey of life and to become to accomplish our dreams. This idea of movement is the trigger for the journey metaphor, as well as for BECOMING IS CONTINUOUS. Conceptual metaphors play a crucial role in organizing information in Michelle Obama's autobiography, they mix together and succeed to structure and orient ideas towards a specific goal, that of encouraging her readers to follow her example.

Another conceptual metaphor of becoming is related to one's pathway in life – BECOMING IS FINDING YOURSELF. The author implies the idea of searching for her own self both during her adaptation to her political status as the First Lady, as well as the ceasing point of that period, when she had to return to her old life.

> *"...when you walk out the door that last time from the world's most famous address, you're left in many ways **to find yourself again**."* (17)

Thus, the concept of becoming is reversed, and the implicit semantic markers [+CHANGE, +PROCESS, +TRANSFORMATION] and most importantly [+FORWARD MOVEMENT] become a turning backwards towards the past version of the person within the process of becoming. The element that strikes us to link the concept of becoming to the conceptual metaphor LIFE IS JOURNEY is the beginning of the quotation, which suggests a journey on foot – *"when you walk out the door"* – as well as the starting point of the journey – *"the world's most famous address"*. However, "to find yourself again" triggers the view to the past, but taken from a different perspective. The present person is actually trying to find the old version of herself, or, rather turning towards the inner self, in order to find personal balance.

This idea is reinforced in the following fragment, where the process of becoming also implies new beginnings:

> *"I know it's a weird thing to say, but to take a plate from a shelf in the kitchen without anyone first insisting that they get it for me, to stand by myself watching bread turn brown in the toaster, feels as close to a return to my old life as I've come. Or **maybe it's my new life just beginning to announce itself**."* (18)

When confessing in writing about her musical experience as a child, learning to play the piano, Michelle uses the word magic, to describe her thirst for learning. Learning is also part of that particular process of becoming better, becoming different, becoming an improved version of the self. Therefore, in this case, we may extend the conceptual metaphor to BECOMING IS MAGIC.

> *"I learned one song in the piano book and then another. I was probably no better than her other students, no less fumbling, but I was driven.* **To me, there was magic in the learning**. *I got a buzzy sort of satisfaction from it"* (25)

Throughout the story, Michelle Obama keeps projecting the concept of becoming together with the process of learning. Thus, life-long studying and finding the best version of herself, trying to perform at her best capacities and wishing to be among the best of her kind are key ideas of her turning into a grownup. Therefore, the following conceptual metaphor that reveals itself is BECOMING, IS TRANSFORMATION. The semantic markers of the verb *to transcend* [+PROCESS, +CHANGE, +NOVELTY] and those of the adverb further [+SPACE, +DISTANCE, +CHANGE] trigger the metal model of transformation, of becoming an improved version of oneself. The process of transcendence is also part of the sematic sphere of the journey, which is reinforced by the movement forward in the explanation *"to get further"* once more, mapping orientational image-schemas. *To get further* suggests movement in time and implies a positive change, while *filter down* suggests exactly the opposite, to move slowly down to lower levels. Nevertheless, motion implies consistency and coherence.

> *"The idea was* **we were to transcend, to get ourselves further**. *They'd planned for it. They encouraged it. We were expected not just to be smart but to own our smartness—to inhabit it with pride—and this **filtered down** to how we spoke."* (44)

Further, the concept of becoming intermingles with the one of growing up, as well as the implication of a solid foundation, which is embedded in the semantic markers of the verb *to ground* [+EARTH, +BASE, +FOUNDATION]. This is where the research switches from analysing the journey of becoming to the static image of being mature. This break is triggered by the concept of grounding. In this case, MATURITY IS GROUNDING, that is building a foundation on solid ground, or extending strong roots into the ground. However, the author also connects the anxiety of a new beginning which is related to the actions of dealing with a lot of stress, or overwhelming feelings. The description of her first days in High School are connected to the process of growing up, thus focusing on the multiple semantic spheres of the grounding concept. These metaphors support the process of becoming a wise, educated grownup:

> *"At Whitney Young, **I had to work to ground myself**. My initial strategy involved keeping quiet and trying to observe my new classmates."* (54)

The idea of coping with stress, which is implied in the interpretation of the conceptual metaphor MATURITY IS GROUNDING, appears again in the story of High School adaptation. Nevertheless, Michelle Obama struggled with the anxiety of not having the right environment to help her become the best version of herself that was possible. Thus, her question can be interpreted either as BECOMING IS ANXIETY, or as LEARNING IS PERFORMANCE:

> *"What if, after all this fuss, we were just **the best of the worst?**"*

The best of the worst antithesis carries the semantic markers of [-LEADING, -HEAD, - TOP, -EMINENCE] which trigger the author's anxiety regarding her schooling environment that was supposed to create the necessary motivation to achieve her finest potential. The same anxiety is revealed in the following fragment, where the writer keeps wondering if the level of her high school was good enough. The degree of her fear is hyperbolized to fatal disease: DOUBT IS CANCER. The semantic markers of the noun phrase *malignant cell* [+INFECTIOUS, +HARMFUL, +FATAL] lead to the interpretation that fear and uncertainty become cancerous when you let them augment out of control.

> *"Not enough. Not enough. It was doubt about where I came from and what I'd believed about myself until now. **It was like a malignant cell** that threatened to divide and divide again, unless I could find some way to stop it."* (54)

This feeling of not being enough may be translated as a lack of self-confidence, which has its roots in Michelle's perfectionism. Throughout her becoming the early stubbornness and anxiety to be better, to become more accompany her along the story of her life, but the lack of self-confidence is transcended in the end.

The following chapter, *Becoming Us*, moves forward to the real change in Michelle's becoming, which involves her love story with Barak and their life journey together starting from their first shy love encounters to their marriage, their children and their political career. In this line of thought, the first conceptual metaphor that supports the exercise of growing together is BECOMING US IS A DREAM.

> *"Barack intrigued me. He was not like anyone I'd dated before, mainly because he seemed so secure. He was openly affectionate. He told me I was beautiful. He made me feel good. To me, he was sort of like a unicorn—* **unusual to the point of seeming almost unreal.** *"* (88)

> *"...we were now sitting* **at the edge of a giant ocean,** *trying on a version of the future, discussing what kind of house we'd want to live in someday, what kind of parents we wanted to be.* **It felt speculative** *and a little daring to talk like this, but it was also reassuring..."* (96)

In both quotations the target domain of the dream is backed by the semantic markers of the adjectives *unreal* and *speculative* [+IMAGINARY, +FANTASY, - EXISTENT, - CERTAINTY, + HYPOTHESIS, +ILLUSION]. BECOMING US IS A DREAM is part of the conceptual metaphor LOVE IS A JOURNEY. First, because their relationship looked like a journey into the unknown, a sort of a voyage but somewhere at the edge of a giant ocean, and second because it was a sort of a utopist discussion because she had no idea how things would have evolved for them, as a couple. However, the idea of passing is still present, no matter the various ways in which something can move. Actually, the idea of continuity is still present with each step the characters make. Coming from a down-to-earth woman, the choice for the word like speculative, though might enforce the idea of illusion and hypothesis somehow also introduces the idea of hope. It might seem a dream but what she really wants is for them to settle down for a life.

Furthermore, after their relationship came true the target domain of the dream turned into that of the secret. It seems as if Michelle was longing for the dreamy situation and tried not to spoil their sensible beginning. That is how we can further decode the conceptual metaphor BECOMING US IS A SECRET that is triggered by the expression "to keep out of sight".

> *"Still concerned about propriety, I insisted* **we keep our blooming relationship out of sight of our colleagues,** *though it hardly worked."* (89)

We finally come across the conceptualization of love as the target domain – BECOMING IS LOVE – which seems to resist the test of time:

> *"We'd been together a year and a half and* **remained,** *it seemed,* **unshakably in love.** *"* (107)

The domain of emotion can be systematically contrasted with that of human relationship like love or friendship and even marriage. This is predictably followed by the conceptual metaphors BECOMIG IS MARRIAGE, as well as BECOMING IS MOTHERHOOD. This process of becoming that is observed along the story line is highly connected to the concept pf change as it projects the semantic markers of [+BEGINNING, +TRANSFORMATION, +NOVELTY]. Thus, in the following example, the author displays the mental image of motherhood with all the differences of perspective, all the sacrifices and all the changes a woman has to take into account when she becomes a mother. The conceptual metaphor that comes after is MOTHERHOOD IS CHANGE:

> *"... for any woman who lives by the mantra that equality is important, this can be a little confusing. It was me who'd alter everything, putting my passions and career dreams on hold, to fulfill this piece of our dream. I found myself in a small moment of reckoning. Did I want it? Yes, I wanted it so much."* (139)

Moreover, the change of becoming a mother obviously triggers a change in the love relationship dynamics of the couple. Therefore, the conceptual metaphor BECOMING US IS ACCEPTING THE DIFFERENCE continues the list of major changes in the process of becoming within the second chapter:

> *"My goals mostly involved maintaining normalcy and stability, but those would never be Barack's. We'd grown better about recognizing this and letting it be. One yin, one yang. I craved routine and order, and he did not. He could live in the ocean; I needed the boat."* (154)

The climax of Michelle's change in her "Becoming Us" is celebrated by her turn back to the professional fulfillment and her feelings of incompleteness in the role of child career. Once her duty was accomplished and her daughters were on their own paths to school, we come across the conceptual metaphor MOTHERHOOD IS NOT ENOUGH, or rather BECOMING IS A JOURNEY, which is projected by the semantic markers of the phrase *at the start of a new phase* [+PATH, +STARTING POINT, +FUTURE MOVEMENT FORWARD]:

> *"I liked my job, and while it wasn't perfect, I also liked my life. With Sasha about to move into elementary school, I felt as though I was at the start of a new phase, on the brink of being able to fire up my ambition again and consider a new set of goals."*

The conceptual metaphor BECOMING IS A JOURNEY reappears in the flow of ideas again, while the author's need to "start a new phase" paves the way to the third chapter – Becoming More.

The final chapter in the autobiography is basically Michelle's becoming the First Lady. This empowering title represents the blossom of her entire political career but at the same time, it is challenging her ability to handle high responsibilities. In *Becoming more*, the journey of 'becoming' is also linked with the idea of a continuous process, an evolution towards a better self for her family, her country and herself. Even as a mother, Michelle underlines the process of learning for her children and offering/giving... As a wife – she continues to adapt, though humble, through true love she wants to succeed in making a life with another person. When the process has been completed then she becomes, she becomes a person of power who often finds herself being in contrast with a person torn by moments of insecurity and sometimes ends up being unheard. (That is why she chose to write the autobiography – as a proof of her wanting to be heard.)

However, the final part of the book starts with a conceptual metaphor that is worthy of the entire effort which has led to Michelle Obama's transformation, i.e. BECOMING MORE IS SELF-CONFIDENCE, where becoming translates and turning into a better version of herself, while more represents her becoming the First Lady.

> *"Confidence, I'd learned then, sometimes needs to be called from within. I've repeated the same words to myself many times now, through many climbs. Am I good enough? Yes, I am."* (248)

Confidence in one's abilities generally enhances motivation, making it a valuable asset for individuals with some level of willpower. Our author-character builds a model of trained self-confidence by exercising her ability to study, to be better and better at either social role that she acquires. Her effort in determining performance is always accompanied by her motivation to create incentives to move forward. The positive answer to the question *"Am I good enough?"* is the central element of the target domain – self-confidence. This carries the semantic markers [+CERTAINTY, +SELF-AWARENESS, +SECURITY] and it projects the conceptual metaphor BECOMING IS SELF-CONFIDENCE.

The following conceptualisation BECOMING MORE IS HEALTH CONCERN, moves forward from gaining self-confidence to moving towards a pro-active role on the political stage.

> *"Planting a garden at the White House was my response to this problem, and I hoped it would signal the **start of something bigger**. Barack's*

*administration was focused on improving access to affordable health care,
and **for me the garden was a way to offer a parallel message about healthy
living.** "* (264)

Thus, being a self-confident First Lady, as well as a mother, Michelle
Obama tries to set an example and promote a healthy and environmentally
friendly lifestyle. Being a very ambitious woman, she takes every new step
as a challenge and decides to do something she has never done. In
psychological studies, it is supposed that meaning in life supports a more
positive health orientation among people, which in turn is related to more
positive health behaviors and health. This is also part of the process of
becoming; learning is a never-ending process. Being a new step in her life
it is also a part of her transformation, which links us to the next conceptual
metaphor, in the series with which she has organized her autobiography:
CHANGE IS A JOURNEY.

*"A transition is exactly that—**a passage to something new.**"* (333)

Though not as comprehensive as the metaphor LIFE IS A JOURNEY,
the metaphor CHANGE IS A JOURNEY employs a process or the result of
changing, a transformation. Change itself undertakes many transformations
and, seen as a journey; it is a process that takes time. Both *the passage* and
the passing of time suggest motion, a step forward; without change, there is
no progress. Nevertheless, when making a change there is always a
transition from good to bad or vice versa.

Michelle Obama's subliminal message is to never underestimate the
impact of change on ourselves. If we do not try to evolve and if we refuse
to change the things that need to be changed in our lives, we might turn into
an obstacle. In order to prevent this from happening, we should take
advantage of any step forward because this leads to freedom. And who does
not like it to be free? Free of all the burdens of life: FREEDOM IS
CHANGE, BECOMING IS FREEDOM and CHANGE IS A NEW
BEGINNING. All these three conceptual metaphors suggest that we
conceptualize various concepts of CHANGE.

*"I am now at a new beginning, in a new phase of life. For the first time in
many years, I'm **unhooked from any obligation** as a political spouse,
unencumbered by other people's expectations."* (333)

We only live once; we do not have to please anybody but ourselves. Life
is too short to feel hooked. A new beginning is a step forward in the right
direction, again the same conceptualization of motion, also suggested by the

journey. The new beginning, the new phase of life is like a rebirth, a new type of experiences, which provides the grounding for the concept of BECOMING which may also be seen as a new creation. If life were not a journey, we would not feel free to travel through it. The power is in ourselves and though we all struggle at some level to live up to the expectations of others, we have to learn to build/develop our own expectations if we do not want ourselves to get lost somewhere between the way others see us and who we really are.

Michelle Obama keeps reminding us about the journey that we make alone or in someone's company, and about learning. By no means, BECOMING MORE IS A JOURNEY/ BECOMING MORE IS LEARNING (and even teaching her own children) for Michelle, a journey in which she learns again, she gains fruitful experience as a wife, as a mother, as a totally new person. However, she is still an ordinary person given the hopes and the insecurities she feels at certain times. She, however, remains the same person of power:

> *"For me, becoming isn't about arriving somewhere or achieving a certain aim. I see it instead as forward motion, a means of evolving, a way to reach continuously toward a better self. The journey doesn't end. I became a mother, but I still have a lot to learn from and give to my children. I became a wife, but I continue to adapt to and be humbled by what it means to truly love and make a life with another person. I have become, by certain measures, a person of power, and yet there are moments still when I feel insecure or unheard."* (333)

Words like *arriving, a forward motion, a means of evolving, a way to reach continuously* map correspondences for both JOURNEY AND LEARNING as both concepts imply motion and a continuum as well as grounding for the concept of BECOMING. She is the traveler in the two domains (that of journey and learning); it is as if we encounter a metaphor within another metaphor since being a traveler is mapped onto another aspect - being a learner. The process of becoming is the vehicle that led her through the journey, while the road is her course of life. Nevertheless, along the way, accompanied by her family and following their course of life, becoming has led to a different stage. The process/ of becoming has led the journey of life towards the White House and has turned into BECOMING MORE IS A CONTAINER:

> *"**We lived in a kind of bubble now, sealed off** at least partially **from the everyday world.** I couldn't remember the last time I'd run an errand by myself or walked in a park just for fun."* (253)

This conceptual metaphor shows that we experience the world as outside us. Even our own bodies and/or minds may be viewed as containers since the structure of our bodies and minds is similar to the structure of objects. In accordance with this idea, we can say that the bounded areas that set us off from the rest of the world, like the *bubble* in the example above can be conceptualized as a container with a bounding surface and an in-out orientation. The members of the family exist and act inside this space. The container is the space that can be entered and thus, becomes the source domain. The bubble is supposed to shelter and protect the people inside of it, but, unfortunately, it also isolates our protagonists from the rest of the society. For this reason, protection comes with both privileges and sacrifices and that is why it may have positive or negative implications. Yet, for people with highly educational standards and goals to live up to, the changes will always lead to success because they will not leave negativity to get to them. The bubble is not the issue; it depends on how we view the whole picture. Psychologically speaking, the human behaviour is heavily dependent on our experiences while the way we respond to the world depends on our individual backgrounds, and on the experiences, we lived along the way.

The bubble may also be interpreted as a metonym of the type - part for the whole – given our tendency of assessing everything around us according to *the bubble* we live in. In the end, we create our own realities in our unique journey through life. That is why, the process of becoming has nothing to do with being perfect, exactly like growing, it is never the destination but the values acquired along the road/journey. The ground for her optimistic way of being lies in the way Michelle has been brought up by her family. It is in her nature to be full of hope and that is why she is eager to open new perspectives for the ones who are at the beginning of their journey, exactly as she has been encouraged by her family, from an early age, taking into account the examples her parents offered to her.

Conclusions

By writing her autobiography, Michelle Obama succeeds in becoming, from a simple South Side girl from Chicago, a contemporary cultural sign. The three chapters of the book may be seen as an extended metaphor of the way in which her identity is autobiographically fashioned until it becomes a cultural symbol. The book reveals, in a chronological order, the experiences that have shaped her into an iconic and compelling woman; the first African American to serve the role of the First Lady. Her autobiography is a testimony of a modest woman trying to be herself and trying to connect with her future readers to whom she confesses. By sharing her own story, not as a personality but as an ordinary person as she keeps repeating in the book, the narrator finds herself on an extraordinary journey of life. Her book is a map into the complexity of a personality's life, mind and soul. The whole book may be viewed as a metaphor, which stands for the destiny of a South American woman who is brave enough to reveal the changes she has made over the years as well as the changes she had to make to accomplish her dreams from childhood and until adulthood. Michelle Obama explores the meanings of becoming with an attitude and a behaviour that makes the best impression not only on behalf of herself but also on behalf of a race and even a nation.

> *"In sharing my story, I hope to help create space for other stories and other voices, to widen the pathway for who belongs and why. [...] There's power in allowing yourself to be known and heard, in owing your unique story, in using your authentic voice. And there's grace in being willing to know and hear others. This, for me, is how we become."* (334)

This is Michelle Obama's definition of becoming and, even if through her autobiography we may not hear the real sound of a voice, we do hear loud and clear the messages she delivers, we notice the power and strength with which she encourages people to follow their dreams. Her messages are even stronger taking into consideration the relationships between races. That is why her voice is an integral part of her individual identity. This is how Michelle Obama becomes the VOICE of the ones who want to be heard, the voice who inspires people, with her confidence, to become what they really want to be. Throughout the story her voice may indicate a high intensity of anger or frustration but in the end she concludes with maturity: *Maybe we can better embrace the ways we are the same."* (334) For all these reasons her authentic voice is unique and can be heard by anybody who wishes to listen. She has raised her own voice to share her story with other people who may encounter similar difficulties in life. Her book is about hard work, self-determination, optimism, about taking action, about getting results, achievements and success. All these may be viewed as dominant cultural values because they speak about attitudes and beliefs.

Michelle's life is a source of inspiration for everyone. It is as if her "voice" motivates and advices people to be(come) the change they want to see in the world. She is an example, a role model; she succeeded in life; thus, anyone can. She herself is the advocate of hope and change and this is her true calling. All through her book, Michelle Obama endeavours in the effort to support and inspire young people into becoming. Moreover, we come back to another central idea of the book, which is a powerful conceptual metaphor: HOPE IS CHANGE. She knows that *"Hope is making a comeback*. People *are hungry for change* (259-260); CHANGE IS FOOD; change becomes the nutrient that feeds them. People assert a strong appetite for a particular type of food, one that can nurture their thought in the same manner in which the emotional metaphor of change suggests. Food is nourishing, it gives them energy to go own, it is a valuable asset.

This is the way Michelle Obama is mentoring the young generation by delivering them positive, subliminal messages: Believe in yourselves! Don't be vulnerable! Hope! The key-words connoting optimism are: dare, hope and dream. These are the most nourishing and energy-giving substances that can fuel a human mind and soul. Motivation is the key to success. Her vision is wide, the message is clear, changes will not happen overnight but we do not have to give up on our hope.

> *The real change happens slowly, not just over months and years but over decades and lifetimes* (211)

Time is a valuable resource and, learning from her experience might help someone save his/her time. In fact, the changes she underlines may also speak about mentalities. She wants to change the world by changing the way people think, she does not want to leave people underestimate themselves but act in order to achieve their own goals. Metaphorically speaking, her autobiography is an open door for anyone who wishes to learn from her experience:

> *For every door that's been opened to me, I've tried to open my door to others. ... Let's invite one another in. Maybe then we can begin to fear less, to make fewer wrong assumptions, to let go of the biases and stereotypes that unnecessarily divide us.*

The door is here a metaphor for the whole book, which paves the way for those who struggle to attain different things in life but are reluctant or maybe afraid that things might not turn as they should for some reason. Michele Obama wants her readers to be as brave as she is, as optimistic and determined to follow their dreams with the promise that in the end, when achieving our hopes and dreams, we will be able *to become* by following the path that has been destined to us, but with patience and rigor.

References

Evans, Vyvyan., Green, Melanie. 2006. Cognitive Semantics, Edinburgh: University Press Ltd.

Fauconnier, Gilles. 1997. Mappings in Thought and Language, San Diego: University of California, Cambridge University Press.

Gilmore, Leigh. 1994. Autobiographics. A Feminist Theory of Women's Self-Representation, Ithaca and London: Cornell University.

Gilmore, Leigh. 2001. The Limits of Autobiography, Trauma and Testimony, Ithaca and London: Cornell University.

Kövecses, Zoltán. 2010. Metaphor. A Practical Introduction, Oxford: Oxford University Press.

Lakoff, George., Johnson, Mark. 1980. Metaphors We Live By, Chicago & London: University of Chicago Press.

Lakoff, George. 1987. Women, Fire and Dangerous Things. What Categories Reveal about the Mind, Chicago and London: University Press of Chicago.

Lakoff, George. 1993. "Contemporary Theory of Metaphor", in Metaphor and Thought, edited by in Andrew Ortony, Cambridge: Cambridge University Press.

Moon, Rosamund. 1998. Fixed Expressions and Idioms in English, A Corpus Based Approach (Oxford Studies in Lexicography and Lexicology), Oxford: New York, Clarendon Press.

Obama, Michelle. 2018. Becoming, New York: Crown Publishing Group.

Ortony, Andrew. 1993. Metaphor and Thought, Cambridge: Cambridge University Press.

Stern, Josef. 2000. Metaphor in Context, Massachusetts: The MIT Press, Institute of Technology.

CHAPTER 3

AUTOBIOGRAPHICAL COMMENCEMENT SPEECHES: PERSPECTIVES FROM GENRE, APPRAISAL, AND MULTIMODALITY

DORRA MOALLA

Introduction

In its early stages, the autobiography was considered as a 'life writing' (Govoni, 2014: 9) genre operating exclusively within the theoretical underpinnings of literature and mediated solely through the written mode (Anderson 2001). In that period, there was a strict divide between the concepts of genre in the literature and linguistic domains.

The 1980's was marked by an important paradigm shift in genre research pioneered chiefly by linguists like Swales (1990), Bhatia (1993), and Miller (1984). According to this shift, genre is no longer viewed as a fixed text type with static features but as "social action" (Miller 1984: 160). This social embedding of genre has made it possible for genres to be altered following changes in the social context. Accordingly, genres change, proliferate, fuse with other genres and media. Following this trend, the original definition of the autobiography genre as a written narrative of the life of the author (Lejeune 1982) has also been altered (Sinding 2010). Therefore, this genre has crossed the boundary with other media and genres like speeches and diaries. In light of this, the commencement speeches delivered by celebrities, which are commonly given in American universities during the graduation ceremony can be considered as autobiographical. These speeches can be considered as life speaking narratives that share with autobiographies their focus on the life of the speakers in order to inspire young graduates. Despite changes in the views towards the identities and boundaries of genres, the commencement speech has not been recognized as part of autobiography and received little academic scrutiny. This is probably due to the belief that commencement speeches are vulgarization of autobiography, an attitude that was refuted but is still un/consciously persistent. The present study aims to find a niche for commencement speech in the autobiography tradition.

In response to this expansion in the generic identity of autobiographies, the tools for the analysis of this genre have also expanded and the need arose to reconcile tools from linguistics and literature for a better understanding of the meaning potential of this genre (Sinding 2010).

Along with a huge progress in the conceptualization of genres through the focus on their social anchoring, genre research has also expanded in modal realization. Research devoted more attention to the role of modes other than/along with language in the meaning construction of this social event (Bateman 2008; 2014). The present study draws upon this change in generic tradition and tries to situate the commencement speech within the generic tradition through showing that the communicative purpose of this genre is achieved through the coordinative use of several meaning-making resources.

Since the main objective of commencement speeches is to inspire young listeners through expressing the speakers' feelings and articulating their attitudes towards people, events actions and states of affairs, we can situate commencement speeches within the domain of evaluative language and semiosis. Therefore, Appraisal - an interpersonal resource in SFL (Systemic Functional Linguistics) that captures the feelings and attitudes of meaning makers can be a valuable tool for uncovering a wide range of meanings in commencement speeches.

Due to a lack of dedicated research on the multimodality of Appraisal, the present study tries to address this particular gap through exploring Appraisal in commencement speeches- how evaluation is negotiated through the coordinative use of several semiotic resources. It aims to address the following research questions:

- How are commencement speeches divided into communicative stages?
- How do Appraisal categories distribute across communicative stages?
- How do the different modes (language and gestures) contribute to the realization of Appraisal categories?
- How does Appraisal as mediated through the different modes contribute to the realization of the communicative purpose of the genre and the negotiation of the genre value orientation/axiology?

- How do gestural Appraisal and verbal choices reflect the idiosyncratic style of the speaker?

1. Literature review

1.1. The Autobiography genre between the literary and discoursal traditions

The beginning of autobiography as a distinct literary genre dates back to the late 18th century (Anderson 2001). The establishment of a genre in contemporary literary genre owes much to the French scholar Lejeune, who defined it as "a retrospective prose narrative produced by a real person concerning his own existence, focusing on his individual life, in particular the development of his personality" (Lejeune 1982: 193).

Scholars like Lejeune started to consider autobiography as a distinct literary genre that has become part of "life writings" such as diaries, journals and biographies (Govoni 2014: 9). At this stage, literary scholars adopted an 'elitist' and 'purist' view of the genre. Lejeune (1982) strived to eliminate fictive autobiographies in order to retain the purity of the genre. The elitist orientation was also evident in the identity of the autobiographer who is supposed to be an established scholar who has something significant to recount and, therefore, marginalized members such as women and pop stars are discarded (Hewitt 1987). The literary tradition imposed also strict norms on the structure of the autobiography and only writings with a chronological order were considered as autobiographical (Lejeune 1982).

One interesting feature of autobiography in this definition is that the autobiographical text is not a mere narrative of the autobiographer's life but goes beyond this to reporting the stages in the development of the autobiographer's personality (Anderson 2001). This positions the autobiographer as an evaluator of experiences, events and entities (this justifies the use of Appraisal theory in the analysis of the autobiographical genre at hand as it will be explained in more details in section 2.5).

It is worth noticing that one of the main tenets of autobiography in the literary tradition is that there is an awareness among literary critics of the social and cultural anchoring of the genre. The author was viewed as a writer with a goal. The autobiographer should have something important to say and should go beyond a mere recounting of events to regulating meanings for the reader (Anderson 2001). Leiris (cited in Hewitt 1987: 35) strived to make the genre "a literary act"- a writing that does something with language. This view of the genre as an engaged writing with a mission to construct values/ideologies aligns with the objective of commencement speeches, which set the speaker, who is a successful person, as a model to inspire young graduates.

The autobiography genre has witnessed a significant paradigm shift when it aligned with the discoursal tradition of genre. Sinding (2010) challenged the strict divide established by literary critics between the autobiography as a 'pure' literary genre and non-literary genres. Sinding (2010) also criticized the disciplinary boundaries literary critics established in the analysis of the autobiography as a pure literary genre that can only be analyzed by literary tools. Sinding also challenged Lejeune's static and fixed definition of the autobiography and argued that genre membership can change over time. Sinding (2010) suggested to bridge the gaps between the literary and discoursal traditions in the analysis of this genre and advocated the need to integrate the discoursal tradition in the analysis of autobiographies.

The first influence from the discoursal tradition is the concept of communicative purpose - a central concept in Genre Analysis in linguistics. In his seminal work on Genre Analysis in academic discourse, Swales (1990) argues that genres are generated out of the communicative purpose. Genres are therefore rhetorical responses to communicative situations and "perform certain social actions" (Sinding 2010: 108). The communicative purpose affects the structure of the genre and therefore, genres are open to a rhetorical discourse analysis.

The concept of communicative purpose was, however, criticized for being a composite and multidimensional concept that can change in different rhetorical situation, the physical context of communication, the participants, the channel of communication, attitudes...etc. (Johns 1998). Many scholars refuted the centeredness of communicative purpose and challenged its adequacy in controlling the rhetorical structure of the genre (Flowerdew 2011; Hyon 1996). The role of the communicative purpose was hedged by Swales himself in Swales (2004).

Another relevant influence in the understanding of the autobiography genre is the cognitive linguistic conceptualization of genre. Cognitive linguistics argues that genres are structured according to a schematic frame of thoughts that trigger prototypical responses from the receiver (Sinding 2010). This cognitive analysis is important because it integrates three axes in the analysis of genre: the writer/speaker, the receiver and the schematic structure of the genre. This triadic relationship can be highlighted in commencement speeches: the speakers operate within established cognitive frames and once they follow them, they trigger prototypical responses from the audience (applause, laughter, admiration...etc.).

Given the critics to communicative purpose, SFL provided a new paradigm shift in the analysis of genre. SFL researchers provided a model of genre that enfolds communicative purpose, register and generic structure. From 1980, the Sydney school of SFL pioneered by Martin (2000a; 2009) established genre as a new patterning of language use. Martin and White (2005: 32) defined genre as "a staged goal-oriented social process" which is translated into "a system comprising a configuration of field, mode and tenor selections, which enfold in recurring stages of discourse". The social embedding of genre is highlighted in the fact that genre producers share genres with other people in social context (Miller 1984). Due to their social embedding, genres are goal-oriented. Genre producers get something done with a text and they typically follow predictable communicative stages to achieve this goal (Swales 1990).

Genre is a variation in language use that is tied to shifts in register components that include selections in field, tenor and mode. Field refers to changes in institutionalized situations and practices across genres. Tenor refers to shifts in social relationships and mode pertains to changes in the channel of communication (spoken versus written) and accompanying modalities (gestures, speech, visuals…etc.) (see Thompson 2014: 39-41).

The present study adheres to the SFL tradition and tries to show that commencement speeches have specific configurations of field, tenor, mode, communicative purpose and communicative stages. In communicative situation, the speaker shares experiences with the audience to inspire them and, therefore, both interactants engage in a very specific tenor relationship. This relationship is also regularized by the institutional practices and constraints of this field (the university institution). This specific communicative context imposes constraints on roles, practices of production, expectations about the content of the genre, the structure of associated discourse and the configuration of communicative stages. Being delivered as a live performance, the commencement speech has a specific mode feature with accompanying modalities such as gestures, pitch, along with speech. The aim of the present study is to show how the modality of gestures coordinates with speech to fulfill the underlying purpose of the genre and how they distribute across the communicative stages to build up discourse texture.

As far as Appraisal is concerned, we are interested in how evaluation is used to achieve the goal of the genre and how evaluation is achieved and distributed across the communicative stages of the genre. In generic structure, we are interested how Appraisal is achieved through the conjunctive use of language and other modes. The chapter is also concerned with showing how speakers exploit Appraisal mediated through language and other modes to convey feelings and attitudes across the stages and negotiate power and solidarity connections with the listeners.

1.2. Genre and multimodality

The term Multimodality has been coined to refer conjointly to a reality marked by the proliferation of modes of representation and to a field of study launched in the 1990's thanks to two seminal works (Kress and van Leeuwen 1996; O'Toole 1994) focusing on the development of methods and approaches to analyse all forms of communication. Researchers in Multimodality start from the premise that modes of representation have expanded in contemporary oral and written communication. Researchers, therefore, argue for the need to devise models for document analysis that go beyond the analysis of the verbal realizations (Bateman 2008) to analyse how modes are orchestrated (Bateman 2008; 2014; Kress and van Leeuwen 1996) Among these models, two overlapping traditions can be distinguished (O' Halloran 2011): the generic tradition and the social semiotic tradition.

The generic tradition is chiefly pioneered by scholars like Bateman (2008) and Stöckl (2015). They tried to develop analytical models to analyse mode connectedness. The generic tradition focuses on the generic, cognitive and rhetorical patterns of mode integration to show that different modes build up discourse texture. Their research direction is deeply anchored within the discoursal tradition of Genre Analysis mentioned in the previous section. They argue that genres are constructed out of a set of social practices. These practices constitute social constraints that build up the document medium, layout, design production and technologies. This generic tradition provided analytical tools for the analysis of different layers of mode orchestration. These models can be subdivided into the following types:

- Content connectedness: how modes connect to convey different or complementary propositional content (O' Halloran 2011; Ledin and Machin 2019)
- Generic connection: how modes connect to realize the communicative stages of the genre
- Rhetorical connections: how modes combine to convey different or complementary rhetorical relationships such as cause effect, general specific…etc.

- Layout: how modes are positioned in the layout of written documents (Hiippala 2014; Bateman 2008).
- Textual: how modes connect according to coherence and cohesion patterns (Stöckl 2015)

The second research direction operates within the theoretical underpinnings of social semiotics, which was chiefly pioneered by Kress and van Leeuwen in the field of Multimodality. Scholars in this tradition devised a modelling of the semiotic resource. According to this tradition, different semiotic resources such as visuals, gestures or gaze are modelled into systems of choices or meanings that are metafunctionally organized (representational, interactional, compositional). Each mode fulfils three metafunctions and each mode represents a system of choices for the realization of one function or the three above-mentioned functions (Kress and van Leeuwen 1996).

The present study draws upon the two research directions for the analysis of gestures in commencement speeches. As far as the first research direction is concerned, focus is laid upon the way modes integrate to convey Appraisal categories within communicative stages (for instance, how gestures combine with the verbal text to realize affect in the opening of a speech). The present study draws upon the social semiotic tradition in Multimodality in the taxonomies of gestures (representational, interpersonal gestures mentioned in section 3).

1.3. Multimodality in audio-visual genres

We are living in a highly-mediated world. We witness an expansion in the media forms- "the means through which the multimodal phenomena materialize (e.g., newspapers, television, computer, material object and event" (O' Halloran 2011: 121). The new emerging media afford a high concentration of modes hierarchically divided into core modes including image (static and moving), language (writing, animated writing and speech, sound and music), peripheral modes such as typography and layout and sub-modes such as size, distance, angle, perspective, gesture, posture, body language …etc. (Stöckl 2004: 12-13). Starting from this classification, we can consider commencement speeches as part of audio-visual media because they include modes from different types (image, speech, sound, music, gesture, posture, and body posture). Since these speeches are mediated through the internet, we can notice a proliferation of modes to include distance, camera movement and perspective. This media transfer from stage to screen is also accompanied by the expansion of viewers and thus the commencement speech becomes a more popular genre. It is true that this genre has a wide reach among viewers; it is, however, a non-transparent domain as to mode configuration and the resources and mechanisms of opinion construction and value negotiation.

Very much like other audio-visual genres, the meaning potential of the commencement speech cannot be deciphered through verbal models of analysis. Many research directions in Multimodality have devised models for multimodal text analysis (the generic and metafunctional models were explained in the previous section). In the context of analysis of multimodal artefacts, Ledin and Machin (2019) introduced a pertinent view. The researchers challenged the systematic application of SFL-based system networks of modes to study all forms of communication ranging from print pages to music. They criticized the suitability of the three-dimensional analysis of genres with intricate meanings and opted for a thematic and context-based analysis of texts. Ledin and Machin (2019) argued for a more selective choice of tools and metafunctions that are more suitable for the analysis of a particular theme.

The present study is aligned with the argument advanced by the researchers. This chapter argues that commencement speeches are interpersonal phenomena involving a direct contact between speaker and audience. This genre is, therefore, more amenable to an interpersonal analysis focusing on the semiotic resources that realize the tenor relationships between speaker and audience. Appraisal theory that will be introduced in details in section 2.5 is considered as a resource for the construction of interpersonal meanings. This theory outlines what is interpersonal in discourse and conveys how writers and speakers construct feelings and attitudes to shape receivers' opinions and values (Martin and White 2005).

1.4. Gestures in multimodality

The previous section has tried to show that the development of audio-visual genres has enlarged the semiotic resources for meaning construction through the synergy of language, sounds, gestures, gaze…etc. Starting from this premise, researchers have become intrigued about how these modes contribute to meaning. They have developed systematic modelling of modes such as gestures (Lim 2017; Martinec 2004).

In his modelling of gestures, Martinec (2004) criticized the view that gestures are holistic constituents that cannot be broken into building blocks (see Kendon 1981). He also challenged the view that postulates that gestures are instantiations of the style of individuals (see McNeil 1992).

Starting from the above-mentioned positions, Martinec (2004) argues that when gestures co-occur with speech, they do not only convey a wide range of meanings but also these gestures, very much like the rules of syntax, can be decomposed into separate meaningful units. Lim (2017) built up on this view and focused on the meaning driven classification. He provided a framework for the annotation of gestures based on the metafunctional classification of SFL. Lim (2017) therefore divided gestures into ideational, interpersonal and textual meanings. He used Appraisal framework to decode and annotate interpersonal gestures. The main weakness of his classification is that he divided attitudinal gestures into positive and negative gestures while they actually convey a much wider range of meanings covering both feelings and evaluation.

The present study embraces the methodology adopted by Martinec (2004) through focusing on how gestures co-occur with speech. In conformity with Martinec (2004), this research study argues that gestures can be broken down into building blocks and their constituent elements are combined with speech to realize one or more constituents of Appraisal (Appraisal, appraiser, appraised).

1.5. An Overview of Appraisal Theory

Martin and White (2005) introduce Appraisal as interpersonal resources in language for modelling the subjective presence of the writer/speaker and the attitude they adopt towards what they communicate. In this endeavour to construct texts, writers and speakers construct not only feelings but also position themselves in connection with "entities, happenings and state of affairs with which texts are concerned" (Martin and White 2005: 2). The present chapter argues that the study of Appraisal is a valuable tool to capture the resources employed by the speakers to express feelings and articulate attitudes in commencement speeches and to uncover a wide range of meanings in this genre. The study of the speaker's evaluation resources is important for the following three reasons:

- Commencement speeches involve a direct contact between speaker and audience that engage into interpersonal relationships, which is the domain of Appraisal.
- The commencement speech, which occurs during graduation day is a situation full of emotions for both speaker and audience and it is, accordingly, hypothesized that this genre is full of semiotic resources to convey feelings, and, therefore, there is a need for the application of a reliable, theoretically grounded framework to

capture the construction of feelings. The present study argues that the Appraisal framework, an expansion of Systemic Functional Linguistics (SFL) that focuses on evaluative language and interpersonal meaning, can discern the interplay between modes for attitude construction.

- The speaker stands as an ethical and social model for the audience. Therefore, speakers try to construct attitudes and values towards events, people and entities to activate the listeners' stance and attitudes.

Appraisal was chiefly developed by the scholars within the Australian school of SFL (Iedema 1995; Martin 2000b; Martin and White 2005). Therefore, this approach draws upon the SFL paradigm. By means of a brief review of SFL, this chapter will try to highlight how Appraisal is anchored in SFL's model of language and social context (Halliday, 1978, Halliday and Matthiessen, 2004).

SFL provides a multifaceted model of language use that argues that in every act of communication language maps simultaneously three types of meanings, which are:

Ideational meanings: this function is concerned with "goings on" (Bloor and Bloor 1995: 110), which include people, events, states and actions…etc.

Textual meanings are concerned with "information flow" (Martin and White 2005: 7)

Interpersonal meanings are concerned with enfolding and "negotiating" social relations- how people interact and share values (Martin and White 2005: 8).

Appraisal is deeply linked with interpersonal meanings. Martin and White (2005) have pointed out that up to the 1990's, interpersonal meanings were confined to the study of interaction (Halliday, 1992). Through the study of mood and modality in turn-taking Martin and other researchers wanted to uncover a wider range of interpersonal meanings by adopting a lexis-based perspective to include evaluation within the realm of interpersonal meanings (Iedema 1995; Martin 2000b)

Another relevant concept in SFL's model of language is realization. Language is viewed as a stratified semiotic system (Halliday and Matthiessen 2004). The first stratum is the lowest level of realization. It includes phonology, rhythm and intonation in spoken language and graphology in written language. Lexicogrammar is the second level of stratification. It is an abstract level of realization composed of grammar and lexis ranked from words to clauses. The third level of abstraction is discourse semantics. It refers to meanings beyond the clause. Appraisal is situated within discourse semantics because evaluation goes beyond the boundary of grammatical categories and builds up in discourse. (Halliday and Matthiessen 2004; Martin and White 2005). Despite the fact that evaluation is associated with discourse semantics, the construction of feelings and opinions is realized at the different strata. Phonology, for instance, contributes to evaluation by different features of voice quality. Evaluation can also be realized by different lexicogrammar categories such as adjectives, mood, processes, adjuncts...etc.

Although SFL acknowledges the importance of the expression domain (phonology, rhythm, stress... etc.) in evaluation, it is a common belief among SFL researchers that other modalities are "attendant modalities" (Martin and White 2005: 7) that accompany language but do not contribute to evaluation in themselves. Very few studies tackled the issue of evaluation in spoken discourse and focused on the semiotic resources of pitch and rhythm as means of evaluation (Eggins and Slade 1997).

The present study argues that against the backdrop of unprecedented development of communication and Multimodality, it is important to expand the study of Appraisal beyond language to seek how different semiotic resources contribute to evaluation. The present study will try to explore how language and other semiotic resources (gestures) integrate to realize evaluation. The guiding principle in this study is that the different modes can be of equal status with language rather than subordinate to it.

One of the fundamental principles in SFL is that language varies according to the context of use (Thompson 2014). Social context is therefore projected into as an external model of language use that is parallel to the meta functional model (Martin and White 2005). This model of language use is subsumed into the cover term register, which includes three categories: field, tenor and mode. Field, which parallels with the ideational metafunction, refers to "discourse patterns that realize the domestic or institutionalized activity that is going on" (Martin and White 2005: 27). Mode refers to the channel of communication (oral or written) and the corresponding discourse texture (Thompson 2014). Tenor is the component of register most relevant to Appraisal. It refers to the social relations as echoed in discourse (Halliday 1985).

The present study posits that evaluation is sensitive to register categories and this can be mirrored in different genres such as the commencement speeches. As far as field is concerned, commencement speeches are institutionalized discourse patterns occurring in a specific institutional context (universities). Appraisal as a very important constituent of discourse semantics, can be shaped by the institutionalized context. Poynton (1985) equated tenor relationships with power and solidarity. Appraisal, as a resource for the construal of tenor, can be used for the construal of power and solidarity. Commencement speeches can be contexts where power and solidarity are expressed in connection with different participants, events and entities through the processes of affect expression and value construction.

After this summary of several cornerstones in SFL theory that tried to situate Appraisal within the SFL paradigm, I will proceed by outlining the different categories of Appraisal. As previously mentioned, Appraisal is evaluation in language, which is concerned with mapping feelings and attitudes – a framework that goes beyond recording emotions – the reactions we are born with – to sourcing feelings and attitudes. Martin and White (2005, 34-39) classify Appraisal into three interrelated domains that are:

- Attitude: it is concerned with the resources for constructing feelings and emotional reactions
- Engagement: it is centered upon resourcing attitudes and the articulation of voice
- Graduation: it focuses on grading feelings and attitudes through the resources of "amplifying and blurring" (Martin and White 2005: 35).

The present study will focus on attitude. Attitude encompasses the construal of both emotions and attitudes and it is divided into the following components: (Martin and White 2005: 38):

Affect
Judgement
Appreciation

Affect focuses on the resources for constructing and modelling emotional reactions of participants in relation to events. It records both positive and negative feelings such as happiness, sadness, anxiety, interest, boredom...etc. The realization of affect is done with a range of lexicogrammar resources such as the modification of participants, processes (mental and behavioral) and modal adjuncts. The following examples in Table 1 taken from Martin and White (2005, 46) illustrate this.

TABLE 1. Realizations of affect in English (adopted from Martin and White 2005: 46)

Categories	Divisions	Examples	Lexicogrammar
Affect as quality	Describing participants	A **sad** captain.	Epithet
	Attributed to participants	The captain was **sad.**	Attribute
	Manner of processes	The captain left **sadly.**	circumstance
Affect as process	Affective mental	His departure **upset** him. He **missed** them.	Process (effective) Process (middle)
	Affective behavioral	The captain **wept.**	Process
Affect as comment	Desiderative	**Sadly**, he had to go.	Modal adjunct

Judgement is more concerned with institutionalized community values. It encompasses the resources for assessing the behavior of people and this is done in connection with pre-established norms and values. It records behaviors such as disgust, admiration, condemnation…etc. Martin and White (2005: 53) assess behavior from two perspectives:

- Social esteem: normality (how normal someone is) capacity (how capable someone is) tenacity (how resolute someone is)
- Social sanction: veracity (how truthful someone is) propriety (how ethical someone is)

The third component of attitude in Appraisal is appreciation. It focuses on the resources for constructing the value of things both natural and semiosis. Appreciation is also concerned with community values. It is concerned with our reaction to things "Do they catch our attention?" appeal "Do they please us?" and composition "balance and complexity" and value "how innovative they are".

In addition to attitudes (affect, judgement and appreciation), Appraisal includes a second dimension, which is engagement. Engagement is concerned with mapping the resources for positioning the speaker in connection with the value position being advanced. This is realized by the resources of projection (for example, it is true), polarity (never, negation), adjuncts (obviously, of course...etc.) and comment clauses (for example, to be frank with you).

The present study posits, as it has been argued for, that commencement speeches are potentially rich with Appraisal categories that are employed to construct the speaker's feelings, attitudes and voice towards participants, events and states of affairs. This study will track down the distribution of Appraisal categories across the communicative stages of the genre and will focus on the lexicogrammar resources for the realization of evaluation.

Given the fact that audiovisual genres like commencement speeches are rich multimodal domains, this genre has enlarged the repertoire of evaluation construal beyond purely verbal semantic resources. This study will try to explore how the verbal realization of Appraisal coordinates with other modalities (gesture) to consolidate Appraisal categories or to express independent Appraisal meanings.

This study aligns with current research studies on the use of evaluation in multimodal genres. Wu (2020) showcased the role of visual, acoustic and verbal modes to convey attitudes for the analysis of video clips. The analysis of Appraisal in Multimodality remains limited because it was confined to mode typology and associating each type with its affordance – its potential to express certain Appraisal categories (for example, the capacity of pictures to express affect). Cunningham (2017) also adopted the affordance-based framework and conducted a comparative analysis of the role of the modes of writing and screencast video in the evaluation of students' writings. Despite the growing importance of different modes in meaning-making, research on the multimodality of evaluation remains scarce. This is surprising because evaluation is an important element in interpersonal meanings. Appraisal theory can represent a robust theoretical grounding for discerning the range of resources of evaluation construction.

The present study maintains that the use of modes for evaluation and the way they fit into generic texture is conditioned by genre type and field. Therefore, the study of multimodal evaluation in commencement speeches can yield genre-specific features. The affordance approach for the study of modes in evaluation is not relevant for the present study; focus is rather laid on how modes are cohesively combined to carry out this function.

2. Methodology

Five commencement speeches delivered by celebrities during the graduation ceremony in American universities are selected in the present study. The speeches are listed below:

- Steve Jobs speech delivered in Stanford University (Jobs 2005)
- Meryl Streep's speech delivered in Colombia University (Streep 2010)
- Oprah Winfrey's speech delivered in Harvard (Winfrey 2013)
- Michelle Obama's speech delivered in Tuskegee University (Obama 2015)
- Barack Obama's speech delivered at Howard University (Obama 2016)

The speeches were delivered by celebrities from different domains (acting, politics and TV shows). The transcript of each video was also collected. Each transcript was divided into the following communicative stages:

- Introductory statement: The speaker greets the audience and expresses happiness to be present in the ceremony.
- Autobiography: the speaker chooses to talk about his/ her life experience.
- Morality: the speaker states the morality s/he draws from the good and bad experiences.
- Course of action by the speaker: the speaker states how his life experience changed his/ her behavior.
- Course of action by the audience: building on his/ her own experience, the speaker advises the graduates about the most appropriate behavior.
- Closing statement: the speaker reiterates his/her happiness to be in the ceremony and thanks the audience.

After dividing the transcripts into communicative stages, the Appraisal categories in each stage were highlighted and annotated according to the taxonomy provided by Martin and White (2005): affect, judgement, and appreciation.

The clause is considered the boundary of each appraisal text. If one clause includes more than a wording of Appraisal, they are considered as one Appraisal unless there is a shift in the Appraisal category within one clause. In this case, they are considered as two Appraisal units.

The problematic cases were cross-checked by a specialist in Appraisal. Afterward each Appraisal category was associated with the communicative stage in which it occurs, its wording and realization (the lexicogrammar resources for its realization such as epithet, attribute, process, projection…etc.). For each Appraisal category, the appraiser, appraised and tone are identified. According to Martin and White (2005), the appraiser or emoter is the person feeling something whether emoting, judging or appreciating. The appraised is the person or thing that is being reacted to. The tone of Appraisal can be positive, negative or neutral.

Afterwards, the researcher watched the video and made screenshots corresponding to each Appraisal category in the transcript. Focus is laid on gestures (head, hands, fingers and posture). Each gesture is described (for example, shaking heads, pointing out with fingers...etc.).

Table 2 introduces the annotation system adopted in the present study:

TABLE 2. Annotation system in the present study

Stage	Appraiser	Appraised	Tone	Wording	Realization	Gesture
Opening	Speaker	-	+	I am happy	attribute	Stretching hands

In this study, focus is also laid upon how text and gestures are conjoined to express Appraisal. The following system in Figure 1 is devised to annotate gestures. The integration between text and visual is annotated as whole when the gesture replicates the whole content of the verbal text. The conjunction is annotated as part when the gesture represents a part of the Appraisal like appraiser or appraised or other elements like process, polarity, circumstance ...etc. For each subcategory, the gesture is annotated as representation or graduation. The graduation gesture serves as a graduation tool (intensifier or downtoner) for either the whole of Appraisal text or a part of it (appraiser, Appraisal or other). The gesture is annotated as representation when it imitates the Appraisal and turns it into visual form. Textual gestures are divided into enumerative gestures that serve to enumerate ideas and arguments within Appraisal categories or conjunctive gestures that serve as discourse connectors. Interactional gestures are deictic elements meant to point out to someone or something (when the element pointed out to is not the appraiser or the appraised).

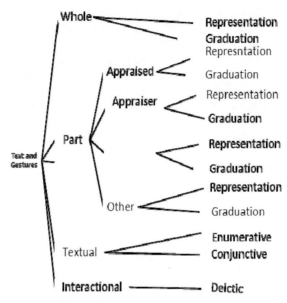

Figure 1. *A Taxonomy of Gestures*

3. Analysis

3.1. Generic structure

The different speeches conform to a standard generic structure. All the
speeches include at least five of the six standard communicative stages.
The only stage absent from three speeches is "the statement of course of
action by the speaker". Each speech starts with an opening statement in
which the speakers express their happiness to be invited to deliver the
commencement speech and then congratulate the graduates. The same
communicative functions are reiterated in the closing statement. The body
of the speech includes four communicative stages ordered as follows:
autobiography, morality, statement of course of action by the speakers and
finally "statement of course of action by the audience". This pattern can be
repeated several times. The autobiography does not follow a chronological
order, from childhood to adulthood. The speakers generally select to
narrate a significant event/episode in their life. Most speakers concentrate
on autobiographical details about their college or professional experience.

3.2. Distribution of appraisal across communicative stages

3.2.1. Introduction and conclusion statements

The introduction section is marked by a positive tone for the different commencement speeches. The three Appraisal categories are present in this communicative stage (See Table 3). The affect category is the most recurrent Appraisal category. It is most often associated with the speaker as appraiser. The speakers express their happiness, pride and honor to be asked to deliver the commencement speech. Judgement and appreciation were used with graduates and institutions as appraiser. These Appraisal categories were used to congratulate the graduates for their success and to praise the institution.

As far as choices in lexicogrammar for each category, the affect category is often realized by adjectives as attribute in a relational process "I'm so glad to be here" (Obama 2015, 00:15). Appreciation is often realized by adjectives as epithet "gorgeous class 2010" (Streep 2010, 00:08). Judgement is often used to congratulate the graduates "congratulations class x".

Despite the general consistency in the realization of Appraisal categories, certain choices in lexicogrammar reflect the idiosyncratic style of the speaker. In his speech, Obama (2016) uses mental processes of affection to convey affect "You cheered them on" (Obama 2015, 01:27). Winfrey (2013, 00:31) uses metaphorical language for judgement "with a special bow".

TABLE 3.   Distribution of Appraisal elements in the opening statement stage and grammatical realizations

	Appraisal	Appraiser	Appraised		Grammatical realizations				
		Sp_1	Sp	Oth_2	Att_3	E_4	P_5	N_6	Other
Affect	17	17	13	4	10	1	2	2	1
Appreciation	4	4	0	4	2	0	1	4	0
Judgement	8	8	1	7	1	4	0	0	0
Total	29	29	14	15	13	5	3	6	1

$_1$= speaker; $_2$= other ; $_3$=attribute ; $_4$=epithet; $_5$= process; $_6$= noun

Table 4 shows that the concluding statement stage has similar features with the introduction in the frequency of Appraisal categories. The main difference between the two stages is that the introductory statement includes more numerous Appraisal categories than the concluding statement.

TABLE 4. Distribution of Appraisal elements in the concluding statements stage and grammatical realizations

	Appraisal	Appraised		Tone		Grammatical realizations				
		Sp₁	Oth₂	+	-	Att₃	E₄	P₅	N₆	Other
Affect	6	5	1	6	0	4	0	2	0	0
Appreciation	3	0	3	3	0	3	0	0	0	0
Judgement	5	0	5	5	0	1	0	0	4	0
Total	14	5	9	14	0	8	0	2	4	0

₁= speaker; ₂= other; ₃=attribute ; ₄=epithet; ₅= process; ₆= noun

3.2.2. Autobiography stage

The autobiography stage witnesses the highest concentration of Appraisal categories. Table 5 shows no significant differences in the distribution of the different Appraisal types. The same tendency is also displayed in the distribution of Appraisal elements and the tone of Appraisal. In grammatical realization, the attribute and the use of process types (verbs) are the most common means to express affect and judgement. Affect is often the use of process types as example 1 shows. This grammatical choice may be exploited to highlight the impact of certain events in the speakers' life on their feelings.

> (1) I **felt** quieted (Affect/ Streep 2010, 9:48)
>   I **stopped succeeding** (Judgement/ Winfrey 2013, 6:32)

TABLE 5. Distribution of Appraisal elements in the autobiography stage and grammatical realizations

	Appraisal	Appraiser		Tone		Grammatical realizations				
		Sp₁	Oth₂	+	-	Att₃	E₄	P₅	N₆	Other
Affect	6	5	1	6	0	4	0	2	0	0
Appreciation	3	0	3	3	0	3	0	0	0	0
Judgement	5	0	5	5	0	1	0	0	4	0
Total	14	5	9	14	0	8	0	2	4	0

₁= speaker; ₂= other ; ₃=attribute ; ₄=epithet; ₅= process; ₆= noun

3.2.3. Morality stage

The morality stage often comes directly from each part of the autobiographical stage. This morality stage is marked by the dominance of affect and judgement (see Table 6). In this stage, the 'other' as appraiser is more common than the speaker as appraiser. The morality stage is oriented towards the positive direction. The grammatical distribution of grammatical realizations is divided into the different grammatical realization with an important concentration of the use of nouns.

TABLE 6. **Distribution of Appraisal elements in the morality stage and grammatical realizations**

	Appraisal	Appraiser		Tone		Grammatical realizations				
		Sp₁	Oth₂	+	-	Att₃	E₄	P₅	N₆	Other
Affect	33	16	19	17	15	9	1	8	15	1
Appreciation	19	2	17	13	4	0	9	1	0	3
Judgement	29	12	19	27	6	0	4	7	9	2
Total	81	30	56	57	25	9	14	16	24	6

₁= speaker; ₂= other; ₃=attribute ; ₄=epithet; ₅= process; ₆= noun

3.2.4. Course of action for speaker stage

The course of action for the speaker stage often follows the morality stage. Since this stage is not found in all speeches, there is a low concentration of Appraisal categories in this stage as shown in Table 7. This may be explained by the fact that the speaker wants, at a certain moment in his speech, to make assertions that go beyond the self.

TABLE 7. **Distribution of Appraisal elements in the course of action speaker stage and grammatical realizations**

	Appraisal	Appraiser		Tone		Grammatical realizations				
		Sp₁	Oth₂	+	-	Att₃	E₄	P₅	N₆	Other
Affect	3	3	0	3	0	1	0	1	1	0
Appreciation	2	1	1	2	0	0	2	0	0	0
Judgement	5	5	0	4	1	4	0	1	0	0
Total	10	9	1	9	1	5	2	2	1	0

₁= speaker; ₂= other; ₃=attribute ; ₄=epithet; ₅= process; ₆= noun

3.2.5. The course of action for audience stage

As opposed to the previous stage, the course of action for audience stage witnesses a high concentration of Appraisal categories. The Appraisal categories of affect and judgement are the most common. As opposed to the previous communicative stages, the appraiser is often other than the speaker and this is quite predictable bearing in mind the nature of the communicative stage, in which the speaker dictates actions to the audience. The grammatical realizations of this communicative stage are varied, but we witness an important concentration of attributes for expressing appreciation and judgement (see Table 8). Another stage-specific grammatical realization is the use of nouns to express affect as example 2 shows. This choice gives a more inherent generalizable nature to affect. We also notice a frequent use of the imperative mood in this stage. This links to the nature of the stage as an invitation to the speaker to adopt a course of action. This is shown in example 3.

(2) **Passion** is vital (Affect/ Obama 2016, 27:07)
(3) **Bend** it in the direction of justice and equality (Judgement Obama 2016, 17:53)
        Feel confident (Affect/ Obama 2016, 21:26)
        Stay hungry stay foolish (Judgement/ Jobs 2005, 14:29)

TABLE 8. Distribution of Appraisal elements in the course of action audience stage and grammatical realizations

	Appraisal	Appraiser		Tone		Grammatical realizations				
		Sp$_1$	Oth$_2$	+	-	Att$_3$	E$_4$	P$_5$	N$_6$	Other
Affect	40	5	36	17	10	7	4	6	14	12*
Appreciation	24	0	24	18	9	20	10	0	0	1*
Judgement	43	5	40	29	14	15	3	7	11	14**
Total	107	10	100	64	33	27	17	13	25	26

$_1$= speaker; $_2$= other ; $_3$=attribute ; $_4$=epithet; $_5$= process; $_6$= noun
*All the realizations of Appraisal are in the imperative mood.
**Ten out 14 realizations are in the imperative mood.

3.3. Appraisal and the communicative function of the genre and its axiology

The frequency and distribution of Appraisal categories are used as facilitator of the communicative function of the commencement speech. As Table 9 shows, this genre is inherently autobiographical. The autobiography stage is by far the longest and the most recurrent communicative stage of this genre. In the commencement speech, the autobiographer engages heavily in the acts of feeling expression and attitude attribution.

In terms of distribution of Appraisal categories, Table 9 shows that judgement and affect Appraisal categories dominate appreciation for all communicative stages, except autobiography. This may indicate that the commencement speech is oriented towards the expression of feeling and the evaluation of behavior rather than towards attributing fixed values through appreciation. This may also indicate that the speech is more oriented towards people (in their feelings and behavior) rather than towards objects, semiosis or ideas.

Table 9 also indicates that the commencement speech is dominated by a positive tone, except for the autobiography stage which witnesses almost an equal distribution of positive and negative Appraisal. This distribution of tone is congruent with the atmosphere of celebration accompanying commencement speeches. The equal distribution of tone in the autobiography is quite predictable if we take into consideration that the speaker is engaged in the act of life reporting events. The negative Appraisal of behavior, values and feelings can be exploited in the following stages to highlight the speaker's success in overcoming problem. This may be considered as a facilitator of the role of the speaker as ethical and behavior model.

TABLE 9. Distribution of Appraisal across communicative stages

	Affect	Appreciation	Judgement	Total
Opening Statement	17	4	8	29
Autobiography	49	43	40	132
Morality	33	19	29	81
Course of action (speaker)	3	2	5	10
Course of action (audience)	40	24	43	107
Conclusion statement	6	3	5	14
Total	148	95	130	

In this process, the speaker stands almost as unique appraiser (articulating Appraisal) and if we omit the course of action for the audience stage, the speaker stands also as the most frequent appraiser (emoter, who is given value and who is being judged) (see Table 10).

TABLE 10. Appraiser and tone across communicative stages

	Speaker	Other	Positive	Negative
Opening Statement	229	14	29	0
Autobiography	76	56	67	60
Morality	30	56	57	25
Course of action (speaker)	9	1	9	1
Course of action (audience)	10	100	64	33
Conclusion statement	5	6	11	0
Total	159	230	237	119

In the commencement speech, the speaker goes beyond being a conveyor of emotions and attitudes to become an ethical model, an influencer who can potentially change the behavior of the audience. The center of Appraisal is, therefore, shifted towards the audience. This is highlighted in the later stage in the speech, notably the morality and course of action stages. These stages witness a high concentration of Appraisal categories. In these stages, the Appraisal elements shift most often to elements other than the speaker (see Table 10). This change in appraiser elements signals an important paradigm shift in the communicative purpose. The speaker shifts from the center of Appraisal to an ethical model, who dictates the feeling, and behavior of the audience. This shift in the direction of Appraisal is also marked by an important shift in grammatical choices. This is highlighted in the relatively frequent use of the imperative mood in the course of action for the audience stage (see Table 11). This shift from the speaker as mediator of affect and attitudes to the speaker as an ethical model of behavior is marked by an interesting shift in grammatical choices. Table 11 shows that the speaker uses a multitude of grammatical choices to realize Appraisal in the autobiography stage and the use of attributes remains the most frequent to express Appraisal. Attributes fulfill a more description-oriented function. The concentration of grammatical choices in the morality and course of action stages shifts towards epithet, process and nouns as shown in Table 11.

TABLE 11. Grammatical realizations across communicative stages

	Attribute	Epithet	Process	Noun	Other
Opening Statement	13	5	3	6	1
Autobiography	56	18	39	21	3
Morality	9	14	16	24	6
Course of action (speaker)	5	2	2	1	0
Course of action (audience)	27	36	13	25	26
Conclusion statement	8	0	2	4	0
Total	118	75	75	81	36

The shift from attribute to epithet signals a shift from attribution of temporary evaluation to a more inherent evaluation. This is highlighted in example 4. The concentration of process and nouns for Appraisal in the above-mentioned stages mark the speaker's strategy to make more generalizable evaluations. This is highlighted in example 5

(4) a **better** story a **better** blueprint (appreciation/ Obama 2015, 22:02)
(5) **The heaviness of being successful** (affect/ Jobs 2005, 7:22)
It improves **the trust and cooperation** (judgement/ Obama 2016, 32:33)

Your class will be armed with more **tools of influence** (judgement/ Winfrey 2013, 18:42)

3.4. A Gestural analysis of appraisal

As Table 12 shows, the use of gestures accompanying Appraisal categories was more frequent in judgement and affect categories and this stands in congruity with the distribution of Appraisal categories in verbal discourse. If we take into consideration that one speaker (Steve Jobs) did not rely on gestures in the realization of Appraisal and that 115 Appraisal instances in all speeches were not accompanied by gestures, it is also worth mentioning that many instances of Appraisal were accompanied by a dense use of gestures at an average of 1.3 gestures for each Appraisal. This may be explained by the multiplicity of the semiotic resources for the expression of gestural meanings (hands, head, finger, and posture). This can also be explained by the affordance of gestures to shift quickly in the meanings they express.

TABLE 12. Distribution of gestural types across Appraisal categories

	Whole		Appraiser		Appraisal		Other		Textual		Interactional (Deictic)	Total
	G*	R**	G	R	G	R	G	R	E"	C¤		
Affect	33	8	2	10	34	15	5	6	5	1	1	120
Appreciation	7	5	2	3	39	8	9	5	5	0	2	85
Judgement	18	2	4	4	41	22	14	6	15	2	4	132
Total	58	15	8	17	114	45	28	17	25	3	7	
Overall total	73 (21.66)		25 (7,41)		159 (47.18)		35 (10.38)		28 (8.30)		14 (4.15)	337

*= graduation; **=representation; " =enumeration; ¤ = conjunctive; () percentage

Table 12 also shows that 47.41% of the total Appraisal gestures are associated with the text that expressed Appraisal content. In counterpart, the frequency of gestures used for interactional purposes (for instance to point out to the audience) is low. The same trend is also displayed in the gestures used to refer to appraiser. This may be explained by the fact that the speaker wants the Appraisal content to go beyond the speaker or the audience. It is also worth mentioning that 21.66% of gestures are connected with the whole Appraisal text. Table 13 shows that Appraisal gestures are most frequently used as a graduation tool in order to intensify the Appraisal (61.72% of gestures are graduation gestures). This applies consistently to all Appraisal categories. This graduation role fulfills several functions such as the intensification of Appraisal content or the whole Appraisal text. This intensification role is often coordinated with sound resources such as pitch and stress. It is, however, worth mentioning that gestures conjoined with the appraiser are more frequently representative (pointing out to appraiser).

TABLE 13. Comparison between graduation and representation gestures

	Graduation	Representation
Affect	74	39
Appreciation	57	21
Judgement	77	34
Total	208 (68.87)	94 (31.12)

Different gestural semiotic resources can simultaneously or successively express two meanings. This is shown in the following example illustrated in Figure 2 (Obama 2016 17:10). The first example taken from Obama's speech shows that the same semiotic resource (hands) can be employed to express different meanings. The screenshot on the left expresses a representation meaning, in which the appraiser points out to himself. The middle screenshot is a visual representation of Appraisal 'too confined'. The screenshot on the left simultaneously expresses a representative meaning and a textual meaning. Closing the hands is a representation of "too invested" while the movement of the hands upward serves an enumerative function.

"My generation"   "too confined"   "too invested in our own biases"

Figure 2. *The Use of Gestures for Several Meanings (Obama 2016 17:20)*

Figure 3 shows that hand gestures can express successively representative, graduation and textual meanings within the same Appraisal category. The screen shot on the left is a gestural representation of the judgement "too loud". The hand gesture in the middle screenshot is a graduation of "too emasculating". While finger movement serves a textual conjunctive purpose "or".

"Too loud"   "too emasculating"   or

Figure 3. *The use of Gestures for Several Meanings (Obama 2015 12:08)*

In counterpart, the same meaning can be expressed simultaneously with different semiotic resources. Figure 4 shows that the representative meaning of "to muffle" can be expressed by head gesture and lowering the eyes.

"To muffle your opinions"

Figure 4. *The Use of Gestures for one Meaning (Streep 2010 21: 48)*

The previous analysis has demonstrated that gestures coordinate with the verbal Appraisal to expand its meaning through graduation and representation. In a few instances, I noticed that gestures fulfill other functions. As figure 5 represents, the gesture is used to narrow the meaning of verbal Appraisal. "Of my goodness" is typically used to express a variety of affect: surprise, shock, amazement, and happiness. The gesture (stretched hands) along with sound features, narrows down the meaning to happiness.

"oh my Goodness"

Figure 5. *Gestures as Specification (Winfrey 00:07)*

In many instances in the different commencement speeches, gestures express Appraisal that is not originally expressed in the verbal text. In Figure 6, the screenshot on the left, shows that the verbal text is a statement with no Appraisal content "I'm in Harvard". The gesture shows happiness and conveys the affect of the speaker. The screenshot on the right indicates that the judgement of Barbara Walters as an important prson was hardly conveyed in the text "I watched Barbara". The meaning is obviously mediated through the gesture.

"I'm in Harvard" (Winfrey 2013, 00:07) "I watched Barbara Walters"
(Winfrey, 2013, 3:47)

Figure 6. *Gesture as independent Semiotic Resource*

Figure 7 shows that gestures can contradict the tone of the Appraisal category in the verbal text. At a first sight, the Appraisal in verbal discourse is a positive appreciation of the speech delivered 27 years ago. The shaking of the head highlights the irony of this positive Appraisal.

"It was really a big hit"

Figure 7. *Gestures and the Expression of Different Meanings (Streep 2010, 24: 45)*

3.5. Semiotic choices and the idiosyncrasies of speakers

The analysis in the previous sections has pointed out the general consistency in the semiotic choices of speakers in autobiographies. Despite this consistency, several semiotic choices (both verbal and gestural) reflect the idiosyncratic style of the speaker. This specificity is reflected in the distribution of affect categories, nature of appraiser, and choices in lexicogrammar. In gestural choices, this is reflected in the frequencies of gestures, their distribution, their types and the semiotic resource most often associated with the realization of Appraisal (hands, head, fingers).

In comparing Barack Obama's choices to Michelle Obama's use of Appraisal, Tables 14 and 15 show that both speakers rely heavily on the use of gestures to express Appraisal. Both speakers rely on hands and fingers for gestural realization. It is, however, worth noting that the gestures of Michelle Obama are most often affect and judgement gestures while Obama uses most frequently judgement and appreciation gestures. The verbal choices display the same trend as the gestural ones. Both speakers use gestures most often for the graduation of Appraisal, which is common to all speakers. Barack Obama uses textual gestures more often. This choice probably proves his argument-based speech. Michelle Obama uses gestures for intensifying the whole Appraisal text. The idiosyncrasies of both speakers were reflected in the verbal choices of Appraisal. Barack Obama rarely uses himself as appraiser. Most often America/Americans are conveyed as appraiser. This consolidates the rational orientation of his speech and his desire to express attitudes beyond the self. On the contrary, Michelle Obama uses "I" as appraiser to reflect this affect-oriented Appraisal. The differences in their axiology of Appraisal are also reflected in their tone and lexicogrammar choices. Michelle Obama uses equally negative and positive Appraisal and uses very often attributes and epithets to realize Appraisal. This consolidates the affect-driven orientation of her speech. On the contrary, Barack Obama uses most often the positive tone.

Another speech reflecting clearly the idiosyncratic style of the speaker is the speech of Steve Jobs. The speaker does not use gestures throughout his speech. His verbal semiotic choices reflect his rational and pragmatic orientation. His choice of appraiser is tailored according to the purpose of the communicative stage. In the autobiography stage, he relies on the speaker (I) as appraiser. In the morality and course of action stages the appraiser shifts to the audience. His lexicogrammatical choices are marked by the frequent use of process types to express affect (I still loved what I did, I fell in love, I found what I loved… etc.). This may consolidate the action-oriented Appraisal.

TABLE 14. Distribution of gestures in Barack Obama's speech

	Whole		Appraiser		Appraisal		Other		Textual		Interactional (Deictic)
	G*	R**	G	R	G	R	G	R	E"	C¤	
Affect	3	0	1	0	3	4	1	0	3	1	0
Appreciation	1	1	1	0	11	3	2	4	4	0	2
Judgement	4	0	1	0	9	4	2	0	9	1	0
Total	8	1	3	0	23	11	5	4	16	2	2
Overall total	9		3		34		9		18		2

*= graduation; **=representation; " =enumeration; ¤ = conjunctive

TABLE 15. Distribution of gestures in Michelle Obama's speech

	Whole		Appraiser		Appraisal		Other		Textual		Interactional (Deictic)
	G*	R**	G	R	G	R	G	R	E"	C¤	
Affect	18	2	1	6	7	4	2	2	0	0	0
Appreciation	3	3	1	3	5	0	1	0	0	0	0
Judgement	11	1	0	1	12	3	4	0	1	1	1
Total	32	3	2	10	24	4	7	2	1	1	1
Overall total	35		12		28		9		2		1

*= graduation; **=representation; " =enumeration; ¤ = conjunctive

4. Discussion

The present study has tried to break with the elitist, exclusively literary tradition in the study of autobiographies. It, therefore, proposed to put under light an under-examined autobiographical genre – the commencement speech. To do so, the present study adopted a transdisciplinary approach that crossed the boundaries between Genre Analysis, Multimodality and Appraisal. In the generic analysis, it has tried to display the standardized organization of this genre into communicative stages. Through relying on Appraisal Theory, the present study has tried to highlight that Appraisal can capture a wide range of meanings in this genre. The commencement speech is an inherently evaluative genre in which the speaker articulates attitudes and expresses feelings. The present study has tried to show that Appraisal categories distribute consistently across communicative stages and display consistent tone and grammatical realizations. The present study has argued for the adequacy of gesture-based analysis of appraisal in the commencement speech genre. This focus on gestures aligns with Martinec's work (2004) in his focus on the coordination between gesture and speech in meaning-making. The present study has, however, highlighted that gestural appraisal goes beyond the expression of positive and negative tone as claimed by Lim (2017). The present study maintains that the synergy of language, gestures along with speech sounds contribute to the expansion of appraisal meanings. In its focus on gestural appraisal, the present study has demonstrated that the role of gestures goes beyond the affordance-based approach adopted by Wu (2000), which postulates that gestures have the potential to express certain appraisal categories. The present study has shown the following roles of gestures in Appraisal

- Gestures can equally express the three Appraisal categories.
- Gestures express a wide range of meanings (graduation, representation, textual and interpersonal meanings).
- In particular, gestures display the potential of graduating language-based Appraisal. Gestures combined with stress and pitch can afford a concretization of graduation of language-mediated appraisal.
- Gestures can allow the visual representation of language-based Appraisal.
- Gestures can express Appraisal meanings independently of speech.
- Gestures can specify/contradict the Appraisal expressed in speech.
- Gestures are potentially capable of coordinating different meanings and different Appraisal categories.

Conclusion

By means of analyzing five commencement speeches relying on Genre Analysis, Appraisal and Multimodality, the present study has tried to show how these frameworks can cross-fertilize to provide a broader understanding of this genre. The combination of these frameworks has allowed to capture the meaning potential of this genre and highlight how this genre realizes its ultimate communicative purpose – to inspire young graduates. The generic analysis has shown that commencement speeches display a conventionalized generic structure composed of six communicative stages used by the speakers to situate the audience within the expected cognitive frame. Thanks to Appraisal Theory, the present study has shown that Appraisal categories distribute according to a pattern across the communicative stages and display specific tones and grammatical realizations. Through this appraisal analysis, the present study has shown that the role of this genre goes beyond portraying positive feelings in the event of graduation to articulating evaluations. This is highlighted in the fact that this genre expresses not only affect but also appreciation and judgement. The present study has shown that the purpose of the commencement speech goes beyond reporting details of the personal life of the speaker to a much broader role in which the speaker sets standards of behavior. This is highlighted in the distribution of Appraisal categories and grammatical choices. This orientation aligns with the traditional role of autobiography: setting the autobiographer as an ethical model and a source of inspiration who negotiates social relationships of power and solidarity. The present study has also shown that gestures contribute to appraisal and to generic texture (see section 4.4).

Despite the overall consistency in generic organization, appraisal choices among the five speakers, many linguistic and gestural choices reflect the idiosyncratic style of the speaker. This aligns with Swales' (1990) argument that genre users follow genre conventions dictated by genre conventions but can produce specific effects.

Despite the fact that this present study has tried to adopt a transdisciplinary approach to the analysis of this autobiographical sub-genre that bridges the gap between several approaches, the findings of this study remain limited in scope. Tis work can be expanded to include other autobiographical subgenres such as diaries or autobiographical novels. The present study can also be expanded by focusing on other modes such as intonation, stress and pitch.

References

Anderson, Linda. 2001. Autobiography. London: Routledge.

Bateman, John. *2008*. Multimodality and Genre: A Foundation for the Systematic Analysis of Multimodal Documents. Hampshire: Palgrave Macmillan.

Bateman, John. 2014. Text and Image: A Critical Introduction to the Visual/Verbal Divide. London: Routledge.

Bhatia, Vijay K. 1993. Analyzing Genre: Language Use in Professional Settings. London, UK: Longman.

Bloor, Thomas, and Meriel Bloor. 1995. A Functional Analysis of English: A Hallidayan   Approach. Great Britain: Arnold.

Cunningham, Kelly. 2017. "Appraisal as a Framework for Understanding Multimodal Electronic Feedback", Writing and Pedagogy, Vo l9, N°3: 457-485.

Eggins, Suzanne, and Diana. Slade. 1997. Analysing Casual Conversation. London: Cassell.

Flowerdew, John. 2011. "Action, Content and Identity in Applied Genre Analysis for ESP", Language Teaching, 44, N°4: 516-528.

Govoni, Paola. 2014. "Crafting scientific Auto/biographies." In Writing about Lives in Science (Auto)Biography, Gender, and Genre, edited by Paola Govoni, and Zelda Alice Franceschi, 7-32. Vor unipress.

Halliday, Michael A K. 1978. Language as Social Semiotic: The   Social Interpretation of Language and Meaning. London: Laden Edward Arnold.

Halliday, Michael A K. 1985. An Introduction to Functional Grammar. London: Edward Arnold.

Halliday, Michael A K. 1992. "A systemic interpretation of speaking syllable finals." In Studies in Systemic Phonology, edited by Paul Tench, 98–121. London: Pinter.

Halliday, Michael A K, Christian Matthiessen. 2004. An Introduction to Functional Grammar. Great   Britain: Arnold.

Hewitt, Lead D. 1987. "Getting into the (Speech) Act: Autobiography as Theory and Performance", SubStance, N° 16: 32-44.

Hiippala, T. 2014. "Multimodal Genre Analysis." In Interactions, Images and Texts: A Reader in Multimodality, edited by Sigrid Norris, and Carmen D Maier, 111-123). Berlin: De Gruyter Mouton.

Hyon, Sunny. 1996. "Genre in Three Traditions: Implications for ESL", TESOL Quarterly, N° 30: 693–722.

Iedema, Rick. 1995. Literacy of Administration (Write it Right Literacy in Industry Research Project – Stage 3). Sydney: Metropolitan East Disadvantaged Schools Program.

Jobs, Steve. "Steve Jobs' 2005 Stanford Commencement Address. "Filmed 2005. Stanford, 22:09.
https://www.youtube.com/watch?v=Hd_ptbiPoXM

Johns, Ann. 1998. "The Visual and the Verbal: a Case Study in Macroeconomics", English for Specific Purposes, N°17: 83-193.

Kendon, Adam. 1981. "Gesticulation and Speech: Two Aspects of the Process of Utterance. In The Relationship of Verbal and Nonverbal Communication, edited by Mary R Key, 207-227. The Hague: Mouton.

Kress, Gunther, and Theodore van Leeuwen. 1996. Reading Images: The Grammar of Graphic Design. London: Routledge.

Ledin, Per, and David Machin. 2019. "Doing Critical Discourse Studies with Multimodality: "From Metafunction to Materiality", Critical Discourse Studies, 16, N° 5: 497–513.

Lejeune, Philippe. 1982. 'The Autobiographical Contract". In French Literary Theory Today, edited by Tzvetan Todorov,193-203, Cambridge: Cambridge University Press.

Lim, Victor Fei. 2017. "Analyzing the Teachers' Use of Gestures in the Classroom: A Systemic Functional Multimodal Discourse Analysis Approach", Social Semiotics, 29, N° 1: 1–29.
doi:10.1080/ 10350330.2017.1412168

Martin, James R. 2000a. "Design and Practice : Enacting Functional Linguistics in Australia", Annual Review of Applied Linguistics, N° 20 : 116–26.

Martin, James R. 2000b. "Beyond Exchange: Appraisal Systems in English." In Evaluation in Text. Authorial Stance and the Construction of Discourse, edited by Susan Hunston, and Geoff Thompson, 142-175. Oxford: Oxford University Press.

Martin, James R. 2009. "Genre and Language Learning: A Social Semiotic Perspective", Linguistics and Education, N° 20, 10-21.

Martin, James R, and Peter R White. 2005. The Language of Evaluation Appraisal in English. New York: Palgrave.

Martinec, Radan. 2004. "Gestures that Co-occur with Speech as a Systematic Resource: The Realization of Experiential Meanings in Indexes", Social Semiotics, 14, N° 2: 193-213.

McNeill, David. 1992. Hand and Mind: What Gestures Reveal about Thought. Chicago and London: University of Chicago Press.

Miller, Carolyn R. 1984. "Genre as Social Action", Quarterly Journal of Speech, N° 70: 151-167.

Obama, Barack. "President Obama Delivers the Commencement Address at Howard University." Filmed 2016. The Obama White House, 45:36. https://www.youtube.com/watch?v=_K4MctEmkmI

Obama, Michelle. "First Lady Michelle Obama Tuskegee University Commencement Address." Filmed 2015. C-SPAN, 26:39. https://www.youtube.com/watch?v=JACTrIRjGos

O' Halloran, Kay. 2011. "Multimodal Discourse Analysis." In Continuum Companion to Discourse Analysis, edited by Ken Hyland and Brian Paltridge, 120–137. London and New York: Continuum.

O'Toole, Michael. 1994. The Language of Displayed Art. London: Leicester University Press.

Poynton, Cate. 1985. Language and Gender: Making the Difference. Geelong, Vic.: Deakin University Press.

Sinding, Michael. 2010. "From Fact to Fiction: The Question of Genre in Autobiography from the Early First-person Novels", SubStance, 39, N°2: 107-130.

Stöckl, Hartmut. 2004. "In Between Modes: Language and Image in Printed Media." In Perspectives on Multimodality, edited by Eija Ventola, Charles Cassidy, and Martin Kaltenbacher, 9–30. Amsterdam: Benjamins.

Stöckl, Hartmut. 2015. "From Text-Linguistics to Multimodality: Mapping Concepts and Methods Across Domains." In Building Bridges for Multimodal Research: International Perspectives on Theories and Practices of Multimodal Analysis, edited by Janina Wildfeuer, 51–75. Bern /New York: Peter Lang.

Streep, Meryl. "Meryl Streep, Barnard Commencement Speaker." Filmed 2010. Columbia University, 28:07. https://www.youtube.com/watch?v=5-a8QXUAe2g

Swales, John M. 1990. Genre Analysis: English in Academic and Research Settings. United Kingdom: CUP.

Swales, John M. 2004. Research Genres: Explorations and Applications. United States: CUP.

Thompson, Geoff. 2014. Introducing Functional Grammar. New York: Routledge.

Winfrey, Oprah. "Oprah Winfrey Harvard Commencement speech | Harvard Commencement." Filmed 2013. Harvard University, 28:58. https://www.youtube.com/watch?v=GMWFieBGR7c

Wu, Ting. 2020. "Reasoning and Appraisal in Multimodal Argumentation Analyzing Building a Community of Shared Future for Humankind", Chinese Semiotic Studies, 16, N° 3: 419–438.

CHAPTER 4

CRITICAL THINKING AT PLAY IN LANGUAGE AUTOBIOGRAPHIES. THE CASE OF INTELLECTUAL PERSEVERANCE

RALUCA GALIŢA & ELENA BONTA

Critical thinking begins...when we start thinking about our thinking with a view toward improving it. (Paul & Elder, 2014: 6)

Introduction

The 21st century has brought an enlarged perspective on the types of competences expected from learners and teachers, among which: communication, collaboration, creativity, creative thinking, critical thinking, decision-making, digital literacy, global awareness, meta-cognition, problem solving and technological literacy. This means, in other words, quality student learning and practice, as well as quality teaching. Reference to quality brings into light the conception according to which teachers are expected to possess the highest-order level of thought, which presupposes being explicitly reflective, consistently fair and manifesting the highest skill level (& Elder 2014). Nevertheless, according to Paul & Elder (2014: 17), "to think at the highest level of quality, we need not only intellectual skills, but intellectual traits, as well."

1. Critical thinking

Critical thinking has become an important field of research in the last decades and specialists in different fields of knowledge and activity highlight its role in individual`s everyday life.

The main approaches to critical thinking come from the area of philosophy and psychology, although many of the researchers in the field embarked on an eclectic approach, both in the definition of the term and in the analysis of the critical thinking process.

The first approach – linked to philosophy – has in view the necessary standards and traits that a critical thinker needs to possess (Dewey 1910). The latter approach, cognitive psychology, is preoccupied with the attitudes, behaviours and skills needed by the critical thinker (Watson & Glaser 2009, Facione 1990). The work of Benjamin Bloom (1956) brought the first contribution to the theory of critical thinking (Duron et al. 2006), by identifying the six levels of cognitive functioning, correlated to cognitive abilities: knowledge (relevant knowledge as retrieved from memory), comprehension (understanding of the meaning of content/previously acquired information), application (applying information in a given situation), analysis (considering the parts of the material gathered and their function within the whole), synthesis (putting parts together in a coherent manner, so that a new whole could be created), evaluation (making judgments based on information). Bloom's Taxonomy was revised by Anderson, Krathwohl et al. (2021); *knowledge* was replaced by *remember* and *create* became the highest level of critical thinking (instead of *evaluation*).

Revising the literature in search for a definition of the concept of critical thinking ends in the identification of a large display of its characteristics, the key words of which are high-order cognitive skills (Facione 1990), intellectual standards (Paul et al. 1997), attitudes, values (Paul et al. 1997), willingness or dispositions (Paul & Elder 2006). All the enumerated elements need to be put at work by the individual in order "to meet the needs of a given situation or at least to improve its conditions". (Uribe-Enciso et al. 2017: 81).

Besides the above-enumerated characteristics, an enlarged perspective on critical thinking also includes other dimensions, as critical thinking is not only the ability to reason well and become independent in thinking, but it also means to have particular dispositions that support attainment of these objectives. Thus, the two distinct dimensions are illustrated by the identification of

1. mental acts and abilities characteristic to the process of critical thinking: consulting sources of information, constructing/evaluating, deciding, experimenting, feeling, identifying and analysing arguments, imagining possible answers, inferring, judging, observing and wondering. Hitchcock (2020) synthesizes the research preoccupations on the issue of abilities and identifies emotional abilities; experimenting abilities; imaginative abilities; inferential

abilities; observational abilities; questioning abilities; argument analysis abilities; judging skills and deciding skills

2. critical thinking dispositions (Siegel 1988; Paul & Elder 2006) – considered as someone`s tendency to do something under certain conditions, in certain contexts:

a) initiating critical thinking dispositions (Facione 1990);

b) internal critical thinking dispositions:

- responsibility
- concern to become and remain well-informed
- flexibility in considering alternatives/option
- formulating issues in a clear manner fair-mindedness; maintaining focus on the issue; intellectual perseverance; understanding others` opinions; willingness to abandon non-productive strategies or to persist in a task, no matter the complexity (Facione 1990)
- anticipating possible consequences
- clarity in communicating
- willingness to revise points of view
- intellectual humility (Paul & Elder 2006).

2. Intellectual perseverance

King (2014) mentioned the fact that much research in epistemology revealed preoccupation for cognitive character traits that comprise "an important kind of intellectual virtue" - *perseverance* – which received, in his opinion, too little attention, in comparison to a large number of studies dedicated to some other intellectual virtues, such as charity, conscientiousness, courage, firmness, honesty, humility, open-mindedness, responsibility or wisdom. This is why his study – *Perseverance as an intellectual virtue* – tries to offer an extended view upon the topic, while establishing the ways in which this virtue is connected with other intellectual virtues. In order to do that, he proposes reflections on this particular virtue, starting from the distinction between moral perseverance and intellectual perseverance and considering the latter as a virtue whose place is between irresolution (identified in the individual`s tendency to abandon too early on his way to fulfilling intellectual projects) and intransigence (identified in the individual`s tendency to continue his intellectual projects in spite of unlikely progress in his work). In this case, he it refers to the tendency to "give up too late or not at all" (King 2014: 3502), based on intellectual dispositions for carrying on the initiated project and manifesting practical wisdom. We could understand out of this that the individual needs such dispositions as being courageous (manifesting open-mindedness, exploring alternatives), being intellectually curious and being persistent in work. Practical wisdom helps the individual to acknowledge risks that are normal on the way of carrying out a project, to find possibilities of managing risks or surpassing barriers and, at the same time, it helps the individual decide when or if it is necessary to stop/abandon the project, as it is not viable. King's idea is that intellectual perseverance is linked to the concept of time and to that of the disposition to overcome obstacles and work hard, until success is obtained. For King (2014: 3512), at the level of conceptual analysis, courage is "a species in the genus *perseverance*".

In his attempt of identifying "the intersection between epistemology and the philosophy of education", Baehr (2019: 447) explored the relationship between critical thinking (understood as an educational ideal) and intellectual virtues (seen as the character traits of a good thinker). Expanding on the topic of intellectual virtues, Baehr focuses, first, on the distinction made by Siegel (1988) between the two components of critical thinking – reason assessment and critical spirit (and then, he mentions the fact that intellectual virtues are at the "heart" of critical spirit); yet, intellectual virtues involve skills and abilities that are virtue-specific and these skills and abilities are based on elements of reason assessment. For King (2014: 3502), intellectual virtues are "acquired dispositions to think and act excellently as one carries out distinctively intellectual activities."

Obstacles that the individual needs to overcome, as seen by King (2014: 3507), are of two kinds: intrinsic (project setbacks on the way of its course, individual's limitations – as far as knowledge or feelings, such as fear, are concerned) and extrinsic (all types of distractions coming from the surrounding environment and that hinder the individual's intellectual work progression). Offering various examples of intellectual perseverance, as noticed in everyday life, King (2014) comes to the conclusion that real obstacles on the way to the completion of an intellectual project are those elements that partly depend on the individual involved in the intellectual activity, with respect to his native abilities and his training, as well as those who depend on external causes, such as time, for example.

3. Methodology of research

Our study is based on a qualitative approach, having as research instrument a personal type of narrative account: language autobiography.

The suggestion for the methodology we have chosen came from the definition that Scriven & Paul (1987) gave to the process of critical thinking; in their opinion, broadly speaking, critical thinking is an intellectual process based on discipline, through which individuals (when/after observing or experiencing the surrounding world) analyse, synthesize, conceptualize, evaluate the information they gather.

Having in mind the definition mentioned above, we considered that language autobiography can play a double role in our study – that is, it can be both the "informant" (offering information based on experience via reflection and critical thinking) and the "tool" ("guide to belief and action" – through its outcomes) – a meaning-making tool (Polkinghorne 1988) – contributing to one`s own development.

The personal narrative, known as linguistic autobiographies, language learning protocols, language learning accounts, language journals or diaries (Pavlenko 2007: 164) can raise awareness, critical thinking and self-evaluation, thus becoming educative devices (Nelson 1997; Bonta & Galița 2011; Bonta 2015), through the attempts of understanding and explaining experience (Burnett 1991: 122). Starting from the idea that it is a good thing for educators to reflect not only on their way of thinking, but also on their experiences of learning (so that they could detect their strengths and weaknesses along the process of learning) (Paul et al. 1990), we considered that using language autobiography as our instrument of research, could help us cover all these issues, in a coherent manner. This is because the teachers involved in our study could analyse and evaluate the information gathered, through reflection, from their own experience and they could get the chance of drawing conclusions and establishing new steps for action.

3.1. Objectives of the research

The aim of our research is proving the fact that the discussion about critical thinking ("at play in language autobiographies") and especially, about the development of intellectual traits (with focus on intellectual perseverance) and their role (within the framework of the need for increased teaching quality) needs to have in view a set of operational concepts, such as autobiographical reflection, critical reflection, reflective learning, reflective practice, teacher as learner, transformative learning, means of improving teacher instructional quality.

The specific aims of the research are:

1) to identify instances of critical thinking during the various encounters of individuals with language learning experiences
2) to identify the steps in the development of intellectual perseverance

3) to identify implications of writing language autobiographies for the process of teaching languages.

Our assumption is that if teachers understand, through critical reflection, the whole process through which they acquired/learned a new language – starting from their goals, overcoming obstacles and frustrations on the way to attaining their goals, they could improve their teaching strategies, techniques and behaviours used in their teaching process (Bonta 2015; Bonta & Galiţa 2011). More precisely, we considered that their acknowledgement of the "steps" taken along the language learning processes would lead to better teaching practices (Strungariu et al. 2014). Thus, in our study, the concept of learning is approached from two different perspectives: a) an individual's learning process – that is, the consistent effort to learn for attaining a (short-term or long-term) goal, involving "risk-taking" and passing through painful stages; b) learning from own experience about how to help others to become good and efficient learners.

3.2. Participants

Our study has in view a number of fourteen language autobiographies written by teachers of English. They identified as fourteen female teachers, nine pre-university teachers and five university teachers. Their participation to the study was on a voluntary basis, within the international project *PLURI-LA – Plurilingualism – Language autobiographies.*[1]

3.3. Research procedures

We have chosen to use a qualitative approach, having purposeful sampling (Patton 2001) as our basic technique, at the level of two analysis steps. A study based on purposeful sampling is logical and powerful, as Patton (2001: 230) mentions, as the approach is based on "selecting information-rich cases".

---

[1] An European project, within Lifelong Learning Programme. Grundtvig (ID 2012-1-FR-GRU06-356503), having three main objectives: educational, pedagogical and social. The autobiographies were gathered and included in one of the final products of the project: Strungariu, M., Galita, R., Bonta, E., Romedea, AG. 2014. *Reflections on language autobiographies/ Reflexions sur les autobiographies langagieres*, Bacău: Alma Mater.

3.3.1. Analysis procedure – Step 1

The first step in our analysis took into consideration the 14 language autobiographies produced by teachers of English, at the level of which we tried to identify instances of critical thinking. Our analysis has two, almost similar, informing sources at its basis: 1) Bloom`s taxonomy (1956) – with reference to the cognitive domain, which includes six hierarchical levels of learning: knowledge, comprehension, application, analysis, synthesis, evaluation, creation; and 2) Bloom`s taxonomy revisited (Anderson et al. 2001) which includes remembering, understanding, applying, analysing, evaluating and creating.

For operational purposes, we coded the autobiographies as T1 – T14. We read them all and searched for the elements of critical thinking, by means of marginal notes that had in view the key concepts of the two, already-mentioned, taxonomies.

3.3.2. Outcomes and discussion for Step 1

In terms of Bloom`s taxonomy (1956), with its revisions offered by Anderson et al. (2001), the critical thinking process displayed in the 14 language autobiographies is easily detected.

Participants to the study manifested critical thinking mental acts, skills and dispositions while acquiring/learning different languages. Respondents narrated about their first contact with languages (in early childhood, in their families; during school years), about the languages studied in formal contexts ad the ones languages acquired in informal contexts. They also brought into light self-taught languages; techniques of learning; stages in language learning; obstacles that they had to overcome; impressions along the way and feelings experienced during the linguistic journey. Respondents recalled facts, people, experiences and "looked at them" with a critical eye: analysed them, explained, compared, classified, interpreted, inferred, defined, asked questions, predicted, estimated or even offered recommendations. The critical thinking levels are briefly presented in Figures 1- 6.

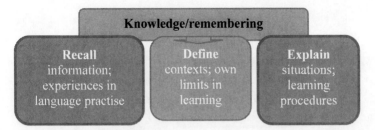

Figure 1. Critical thinking level – knowledge (Bloom 1956); remembering (Anderson et al. 2001)

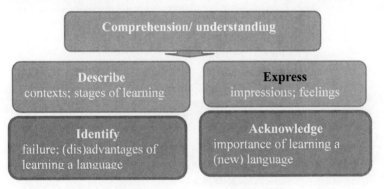

Figure 2. Critical thinking level – comprehension (Bloom 1956); understanding (Anderson et al. 2001)

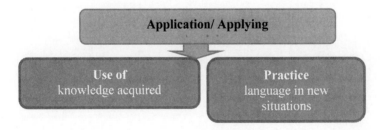

Figure 3. Critical thinking level – application (Bloom 1956); applying (Anderson et al. 2001)

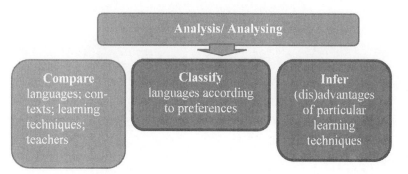

Figure 4. Critical thinking level – analysis (Bloom 1956); analysing (Anderson et al. 2001)

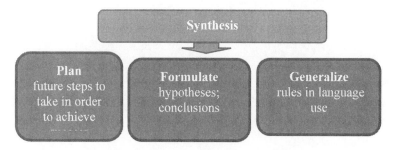

Figure 5. Critical thinking level – synthesis (Bloom 1956)

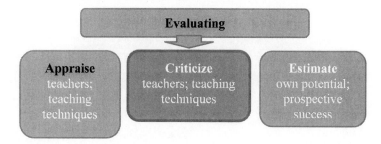

Figure 6. Critical thinking level – evaluate (Bloom 1956); evaluating (Anderson et al. 2001)

3.3.3. Analysis procedure – Step 2

The second thing we did was to use an intensity sampling technique in order to analyse the steps taken in the development of intellectual traits, with focus on *intellectual perseverance*. In Patton's opinion (2001), intensity sampling in the field of research synthesis means the selection of those samples that are

> ...*excellent or rich examples of the phenomenon of interest, but not highly unusual cases...cases that manifest sufficient intensity to illuminate the nature of success or failure, but not at the extreme. (Patton 2001: 234)*

The rationales behind the decision are linked to the rich number of contacts the chosen respondent established with various languages, the number of the acquired/learned languages; the detailed presentation and analysis of each encounter and experience; the clear and detailed way in which the respondent disclosed intellectual dispositions; the clear way in which intellectual perseverance was revealed in the narrative account.

Therefore, the language autobiography coded T12[2] was selected for in-depth information on the research point of interest: the steps towards the development of intellectual traits, with focus on intellectual perseverance.

This time, the analysis has in view Paul & Elder's model of critical thinking (2007), Baehr's (2015) identification and classification of intellectual virtues and, at the same time, ideas coming from the literature on intellectual abilities and intellectual dispositions.

3.3.4. Outcomes and discussion for Step 2

According to Paul & Elder (2007: 2), critical thinking is "the art of *analysing* and *evaluating* thinking with a view to *improving* it".[3] Their framework of critical thinking includes these three important components: analysis of thinking (*the elements of thought*); evaluation of thinking (*the universal intellectual standards*) and improvement of thinking (*the intellectual traits*). According to them, the first component discloses the structures of thinking: purposes; questions; information; points of view; inferences; concepts; implications and assumptions. The second component enumerates the standards that individuals need to have in view when evaluating thinking (the focus is on the quality of thinking): accuracy; breadth; clarity; depth; fairness; logic; precision; relevance; significance and sufficiency. The third element has in view the result of

---

[2] The full version of the autobiography can be found in Strungariu, M., Galita, R., Bonta, E., Romedea, A.G. *2014. Reflections on language autobiographies/ Reflexions sur les autobiographies langagieres*, Bacău: Alma Mater, pp. 65-69.

[3] Italics belong to the authors, for a better illustration of the immediately following ideas in the paragraph.

the efforts made by the individual to apply, consistently, the intellectual standards to the elements of thought; this means that the individual develops intellectual traits, such as intellectual autonomy; intellectual courage; intellectual humility; intellectual integrity; intellectual perseverance; intellectual reason and fairmindedness.

The autobiography chosen for analysis offers a large display of examples of all the enumerated elements and, at the same time, it makes clear the respondent`s entire "mechanism" of thought, her dispositions, skills, behaviour and feelings associated to the process of language acquisition and learning.

The author of T12, just like the other 13 respondents, observes a chronological order of events and begins the autobiography with memories from childhood. The autobiography opens with a generalized view upon the issue, in which its author is honest in confessing unawareness, in an easily noticeable intellectual humility:

> *I cannot say I remember having always liked foreign languages or having had any talents in this regard.*

The adverb "always" circumscribes expectations for a changed future attitude, skills and new feelings, marked by awareness and critical thinking acts. At the same time, the sentence also discloses intellectual humility. The question is: how did the author of this autobiography, starting from this state – openly mentioned – reached the one in which she "discovered" her love, passion, talent for languages, in general, and for English, in particular, and how did she overpass obstacles in order to accomplish the final goal: that of knowing and speaking English efficiently and becoming a teacher of English?

The analysis of the author`s "encounters" with languages and their characteristics, with people influencing these contacts, with obstacles on the way of language acquisition and learning, reveals the following[4]:

---

[4] In order to reach the conclusions, we divided the autobiographical narrative into 10 fragments, following, somehow, the accurate, clear and logical presentation made by the author herself.

Getting knowledge	Languages	Context
Acquisition in informal contexts	Romanian	within the small and large community, as native language
	different Romanian dialects	assimilation through exposure to different Romanian dialects; the contacts were facilitated by the frequent meetings with relatives living in different linguistic areas in the country
	Russian	picking up words and complete structures from members of the family
	English	picking up words from TV cartoons
	Italian	TV programs (for children, entertainment, music)
	Spanish	picking up words and completing structures from soap-operas
	Polish	picking up words during a scholarship in Poland
Learning (in formal contexts of instruction)	German	contact facilitated by TV scheduled courses of German
	Romanian	as a subject included in the curriculum
	French	as a subject included in the curriculum, starting with the 5th grade in gymnasium
	English	as a subject included in the curriculum, starting with the 6th grade in gymnasium, continuing the study during and while attending a Faculty of Letters
	Dutch	during MA studies

In the case of language acquisition, the first linguistic experience that the respondent mentions is that with Romanian dialects inherited by her parents and relatives, who belonged to different geographical areas of Romania. The respondent discloses her observational abilities while making the comparison with the (somehow) standard Romanian language she used to speak at home: "some of the words sounded strange"; they had "a distinct pronunciation" (65) and the contact with them represented a "linguistic shock" for her. The respondent even analyses in depth the differences that she noticed: "...the lexical differences were not very many, but the phonetic ones were numerous. The transformation of both consonants and vowels was very strong". (66)

Curiosity, as a virtue required to initially motivate learning (Baehr, 2015), "a thirst for understanding and a desire to explore"[5], as well as "the desire of learning a new language" (65) helps our respondent to make an effort and try to learn German, by attending a televised course. Once involved in the learning process, she has the chance to get rid of misconceptions – German did not seem to her as a language "with too many rough sounds" (65) any longer. Her confession is a real proof of her internal critical thinking disposition – more exactly her willingness to revise/reformulate points of view while she is narrating the learning experience. She evaluates teachers and their way of teaching – "they spoke "very clearly" (65) and behaving in the classroom –"they were pleasant" (65).

Other experiences with languages in informal contexts include those in which the respondent acquires not only words, but also structures in Italian and Spanish. The common denominators are their source (TV programs – entertainment shows, soap-operas), as well as the satisfaction brought by the ease in the use of the two languages in everyday contexts, during meetings with native speakers of Italian and Spanish.

When it comes about the learning of a language in formal contexts, the first language she mentions and she feels love for is Romanian (which is quite surprising, as the other respondents did not insist too much on the mother tongue). During the secondary school, she becomes aware of her love for the grammar of the Romanian language and even attempts to make "some connections between the Romanian language and its roots in the Latin language" (65), although she mentions that "the whole process of learning Latin was not really appealing to me" (65). The respondent also mentions her experience with the formal way of learning Romanian, proving strong critical thinking abilities. It is the moment when she acquires "a taste for reading" (66), a thing that helps her to take part in school competitions in the Romanian languages (although she was a pupil in a technical high school). At the same time, by maintaining focus on the reading activity, she becomes aware of the unexpected "huge lexical acquisition" (especially neologisms) (66) – a thing that puts to test her creativity: she initiates her "own dictionary" for the new words and their definitions. More than this, she becomes aware of the passion she develops for learning "I was avid for knowing as many words as I could" (66). New feelings accompanying realization are recorded: "I was very proud of knowing them and of being able to use them in various contexts" (66)

---

[5] Intellectual Virtues Academy – available at
https://www.ivalongbeach.org/about/about-iva

French, the first foreign language the respondent was exposed to, made an important impact on her due to the technique the French teacher used – learning for pleasure – by means of songs whose lyrics helped learners to get in contact with the language vocabulary and grammar rules and learn them more quickly and with stronger effects on long-term memory.

The 6th grade meant the respondent's contact with English, the language called by her "my real fascination" (66), the one that she immediately fell in love with and whose proficiency (in terms of words and structures mastery) constituted an important short and long-term objective, at the same time (for both the learner and the English teacher-to-be). She recalls the childhood memories when, "with curious eyes" (66) she used to watch cartoons and then, unconsciously tried to understand meanings by means of associations between images and words. At the same time, she manifests attentiveness, as a virtue required to guide learning (Baehr 2015); she takes advantage of every opportunity in order to clarify meanings. The respondent recollects her contradictory conversations with friends, while trying to get the sense of expressions they came across in lyrics or films. While in class, her "struggle" for understanding and becoming better and better in English, every day, was under the sign of the permanent help received from the teacher and that of her own hard work. The respondent appreciates the teacher who becomes a model to her: she had an accent and pitch that "sounded very British" (66), she encouraged every effort made by the learner and the teaching techniques were attractive. Learners never had the chance to get bored. The respondent makes her decision: her goal in life is established: "If in primary school I had admired my primary school teacher very much and I was determined to follow a job similar to hers, in elementary school I knew I had chosen my path in life as a teacher of English" (67).

While learning languages in informal contexts had curiosity, pleasure, attractiveness as its basic elements, from the moment the respondent discloses that she made the decision concerning her future job, the autobiography reveals instances of intellectual perseverance.

Disclosing the desire of attending a high school with a profile in foreign languages, she hits the first obstacle: her parents would rather she attended an economic high school, as it could have provided her with a graduation diploma meant to ensure her a quicker possibility of employment on the labour market.

The respondent is not discouraged. On the contrary, she clearly reiterates her determination and disposition for hard work, doubled by intellectual autonomy, on the way to objective achievement. This materialized in reading extra-curricular material (books for children), as she felt a great satisfaction "to learn English from direct genuine contexts" (67). The feeling was exacerbated by the socio-political context of the time of her childhood and study years – the socio-political situation in the country: the respondent's childhood and adolescence were under the mark of the communist regime in Romania, which meant a limited number of foreign languages in school curricula, limited or no possibility to get authentic material to read in the foreign language, little or no opportunity to meet native speakers. The fact that one relative of hers gave her some English books to read, made her happy and proud and feel privileged, in comparison with her fellows.

She has the courage to translate one book into Romanian, being marked by the ambition of pursuing her goal. The process of translation proves to be a difficult one, as she has "a primitive dictionary" (67); nevertheless, although that means a new obstacle in the process of learning, she does not feel it like that, as the teacher is constantly encouraging her and the efforts she makes. More than this; she feels very proud of her dictionary, as she is also proud of her compiled list of new words – her own dictionary including the newly acquired words. Open-mindedness and interest in the subject, together with intellectual tenacity are put at work as "virtues required to overcome obstacles" (Baehr 2015).

Intellectual humility (Paul & Elder 2006) marked the new steps our respondent took onwards. Although working hard in English, she does not enlist for English school competitions; she admits she was not good enough for that, either because of her distrust in her own forces, or because that was a problem created by the syllabus of the economic high school that did not offer her the same training that was offered to learners of theoretical high schools. The respondent's confession is a new proof of intellectual humility as she is aware of her own limitations. However, her perseverance in attaining the goal is to be noticed: "I was still undeterred in attending a Faculty of foreign languages" (67). It is this perseverance that makes her teacher of English encourage her in the attempts she takes in the classroom, appreciating her constant effort and love for English. It is her perseverance that makes her parents determined to offer her the support she needs. They decide to allow her to take private lessons in English so that she could progress in her study. Their decision (based on "the effort of paying for some private lessons") helped her a lot and their effort, together with the respondent's one, were worth it; she successfully passed the entrance examination at the Faculty of Letters.

What seems really interesting, is that the autobiography continues and offers us the respondent's thoughts and feelings in her quality of an English teacher; she discloses some of the teaching techniques she applies in the classroom, the way in which she encourages her students to study, but more than this, she discloses the fact that she shares "the same passion for English...and the joy" (68) in its use while teaching. With intellectual humility, she feels "the panic of not having the colloquial use of the English specific to a native speaker" (68) and open-mindedly experiments in her profession each year, so as "to perfect my skills" (68), as she confesses; in other words, she strives to be not only a teacher, but also a quality teacher.

Conclusions

The perseverance in attaining the goal in life our respondent has proved all along her narration, together with her passion for languages, in general, and for English, in particular, make us think of the concept of grit which has drawn the attention of many researchers in the last decades (Duckworth et al. 2007, Duck worth & Gross 2014, Von Culin et al. 2014, Baruch-Feldman 2017, Fernández-Martín et al. 2018, Cormier et al. 2019 or Datu 2021). It means, according to Baruch-Feldman (2017) "the ability to persist in something you feel passionate about and persevere when you face obstacles".

Developing critical thinking is one major goal in both learning and teaching. As far as education is concerned, interest in critical thinking is evident in the work of McPeck (1981), Paul et al. (1997), Ennis (2013), Astleitner (2007), Possin (2008), Uribe-Encio et al. (2017), Pineda (2004), Brumfit (2005), Gelder (2005), Davies & Barnett (2015), and Kraak (2000 – as cited in Astleitner, 2007: 53). They consider critical thinking as the most important of all present educational tasks. This means, on the one hand, that learners need to be taught how to become good and effective thinkers, as according to Paul & Elder (2014), critical thinking must be cultivated. On the other hand, teachers need to apply critical thinking in their teaching activity, as this presupposes reflection upon and evaluation of their learners' steps in learning and achievements, as well as evaluation of their own practice of teaching.

By reflecting on their own experiences with languages, teachers can have the opportunity of changing attitudes, behaviour and teaching techniques so that they could meet the needs of their learners, of the learners` personality and learning styles.

The idea goes the same line with the findings provided by Roberts (2019) who reviews the relevant literature on reflection and identifies four important directions of research on the topic, according to the position researchers take towards reflection. Thus, she mentions: a) reflection as thinking; b) reflection as a voicing in the attempt of getting knowledge; c) reflection as a re-visioning - that encourages "renewed courses of action"; d) reflection as transformation (transformation of ideas, behaviour, action). These directions encapsulate the idea of reflection as a learning strategy.

According to Jasper (2013: 43), reflective learning is a possibility of adding knowledge to knowledge base, as well as changing behaviour in own practice after a process of "reconsidering and rethinking" own previous experiences and knowledge from a variety of angles (Bolton, 2010: 13). Conclusions drawn from reflection can constitute the basis for teachers` learning how they could become quality teachers. We think that our respondent`s autobiography could clearly prove that.

We are aware of the limitations of our study. First, we mention the small number of respondents (n = fourteen) we have worked with, which, however, can be explained considering the objective that we had in mind for the first step of our research. We intended to draw general conclusions regarding the instances of critical thinking in teachers` language autobiographies, without keen interest in intellectual perseverance.

Second, we deliberately have chosen just one sample (although we have not entirely observed the requirements of the intensity sampling techniques), for reasons we have already explained while presenting the chosen methodology. A further study, in which three or four language autobiographies can be analysed with the same objective ("detecting" intellectual perseverance) in a comparative way could bring a better understanding of the problem under discussion and new conclusions can be added to the already formulated ones.

References

Anderson, Lorin. W., Krathwohl, David. R., Airasian, Peter. W., Cruikshank, Kathleen. A., Mayer, Richard. E., Pintrich, Paul. R., Raths, James., Wittrock, Merlin. C. 2001. A taxonomy for learning, teaching, and assessing: A revision of Bloom`s Taxonomy of Educational Objectives. New York: London

Astleitner, H. 2007. "Teaching Critical Thinking Online", Journal of Instructional Psychology, 29, N°2, 53-77.

Baehr, Jason. 2015. Cultivating Good Minds: A Philosophical & Practical Guide to Educating for Intellectual Virtues, available at https://intellectualvirtues.org/why-should-we-educate-for-intellectual-virtues-2-2/

Baehr, Jason. 2019. "Intellectual Virtues, Critical Thinking and the Aims of Education." In The Routledge Handbook of Social Epistemology, edited by Miranda Fricker, Peter, J. Graham, David Henderson, and Nikolaj, J.L.L. Pederson, 447-457. New York & London: Routledge.

Baruch-Feldman, Caren. 2017. What is grit and why is it important? – available at https://www.newharbinger.com/blog/self-help/what-is-grit-and-why-is-it-important/

Bolton, Gillie and Delderfield, Russel. 2010. Reflective practice: Writing and professional development. New York: Sage.

Bonta, Elena. 2015. Understanding Language Autobiographies, Lambert Academic Publishing.

Bonta, Elena., Galița, Raluca. 2011. "Linguistic autobiographies or making sense of one's own language learning experiences. Case study", Philologia Journal, 9, N°1-10: 65-73.

Brumfit, C. et al. 2005. "Language Study in Higher Education and the Development of Criticality," International Journal of Applied Linguistics, 15, N° 2: 145-168 - available at https://doi.org/10.1017/s026- 1444800014828

Burnett, R. 1991. "Accounts and narratives." In Studying Interpersonal Interaction, edited by Barbara Montgomery and Steve Duck, 121-141, New York: The Guilford.

Cormier, Danielle.L., Dunn, John.G.H, Causgrove Dunn, Janice. 2019. « Examining the domain specificity of grit", Personality and Individual Differences, N°139, 349-354.

Datu, Jesus. Alfonso. D. 2021. "Beyond passion and perseverance: review and future research initiatives on the science of grit", Frontiers in Pshychology, 11, article 545526 – available at https://www.frontiersin.org/articles/10.3389/fpsyg.2020.545526/full

Davies, Martin, and Barnett, Ronald. 2015. The Palgrave Handbook of Critical Thinking in Higher Education, New York: Palgrave Macmillan

Dewey, John. 1910. How we think, available online at https://bef632.files.wordpress.com/2015/09/dewey-how-we-think.pdf

Duckworth, Angela. L., Peterson, Christopher., Matthews, Michael.D., Kelly, Dennis.R. 2007. "Grit: Perseverance and passion for long-term goals." Journal of Personality and Social Psychology, 92, N°6: 1087-1101, available online at https://www.researchgate.net/ publication/ 6290064_Grit_Perseverance_and_Passion_for_Long-Term_Goals

Duckworth, Angela., & Gross, James.J. 2014. "Self- Control and Grit: Related but Separable Determinants of Success," Current Directions in Psychological Science, 23, N°5, 319-325, available online at https://www.researchgate.net/publication/280771582_Self-Control_and_Grit_Related_but_Separable_Determinants_of_Success

Duron, Robert., Limbach, Barbara., Waugh, Wendy. 2006. "Critical
    Thinking Framework for Any Discipline", International Journal of
    teaching and Learning in Higher Education, 17, N°2, 160-166
Ennis, Robert.H. 2013. "Critical Thinking Across the Curriculum: The
    Wisdom CTAC Program". Inquiry: Critical Thinking Across the
    Disciplines, 28, N° 2, 25-45
Facione, Peter. A. 1990. "Critical Thinking: A Statement of Expert
    Consensus for Purposes of Educational Assessment and Instruction",
    available at
    https://www.researchgate.net/publication/242279575_Critical_Thinkin
    g_A_Statement_of_Expert_Consensus_for_Purposes_of_Educational_
    Assessment_and_Instruction
Fernández- Martin, Francisco .A., Arco-Tirado, Jose.L. & Soriano-Ruiz,
    María. 2018. "Perseverance and passion for achieving long-term goals:
    Transcultural adaptation and validation of the Grit-Scale", Revista de
    Psicologia Social, 33, N°3, 620-649 – downloaded from
    https://www.tandfonline.com/doi/epdf/10.1080/02134748.2018.14820
    60?needAccess=true&role=button- August, 17, 2022
Hitchcock, David. 2020. "Critical Thinking". In The Stanford Encyclopedia of
    Philosophy, edited by Edward Zalta, and Uri Nodelman. available at
    https://plato.stanford.edu/archives/fall2020/entries/critical-thinking/
van Gelder, T.J. 2005. "Teaching critical thinking: some lessons from
    cognitive science", College Teaching, 53, N°1, 41-46
Jasper, Melanie., Rosser, Megan. & Mooney, Gail. 2013. Professional
    Development, Reflection, Decision-Making in Nursing and Healthcare,
    Wiley-Blackwell.
King, Nathan.L. 2014. "Perseverance as an intellectual virtue," Synthese,
    N°191, 3501-3523, DOI: 10.1007/s11229-014-1418-1, available at
    https://link.springer.com/article/10.1007s11229-014-0418-1
McPeck, John. 1981. Critical Thinking and Education, London: Routledge
Nelson, Alex. 1997. "Imagining and critical reflection in autobiography:
    An odd couple in adult transformative learning", Adult Education
    Research Conference, https://newprairiepress.org/ aerc/1997/papers/33/
Patton, Michael.Quinn. 2001. Qualitative research and evaluation
    methods, ed. Thousand oaks CA: Sage Publications.
Paul, Richard.W., A.J.A.Binker, Jensen, Karen, and Kreklau, Heidi. 1990.
    Critical thinking handbook. 4th-6th grades, downloaded from
    https://eric.gov/?id=ED325804 – August 11, 2022

Paul, Richard.W., Elder, Linda. & Bartell, Ted. 1997. "California Teacher Preparation for Instruction in Critical Thinking: Research Findings and Policy Recommendations" – downloaded from https://files.eric.gov/fulltextED437379.pdf - August 1*7, 2022*

Paul, Richard.W. & Elder, Linda., 2006/2007. The Miniature Guide to critical Thinking Concepts and Tools, Foundation for Critical Thinking – downloaded from: https://www.criticalthinking.org/files/Concepts_Tools.pdf

Paul, Richard.W. & Elder, Linda. 2014. Critical Thinking: Tools for Taking Charge of Your personal and Professional Life, New Jersey: Pearson Education Inc.

Pavlenko, Aneta. 2007. "Autobiographical Narratives as data in Applied linguistics", Oxford Journals. Applied Linguistics, Oxford University Press, 28, N° 2: 163-188.

Pineda-Páez, Clelia. 2004. "Critical Thinking in the EFL Classroom: The Search for a Pedagogical Alternative to Improve English", Ikala, Revista de Lenguaje y Cultura, 9, N° 15, 45-80 – available at www.redalyc.org/pdf/2550 /255025901003.pdf

Polkinghrne, Donald. 1988. Narrative knowing and the human science. Albany: State University of New York Press.

Possin, Kevin. 2008. A Field Guide to Critical Thinking Assessment, Teaching Philosophy, 31, N° 3, 201-228, downloaded from https://www.academia.edu/30748826/A_Field_Guide_to_Critical-Thinking_Assessment - August 15, 2022

Roberts, Kelly.Morris. 2019. "An analysis of autobiographical tools in written reflection: implications for teaching critical thinking and goal-setting", Reflective Practice, 20, N° 8, 201-217

Roberts, Robert.C. & Wood, Jay.W. 2007. Intellectual Virtues: A Essay in Regulative Epistemology, New York: Oxford University Press

Scriven, Micahel. & Paul, Richard. W. 1987. "Defining critical thinking". 8th Annual International Conference on Critical Thinking and Education Reform – available at https://www.edweek.org/leadership/opinion-critically-thinking-about-critical-thinking/2018/06

Siegel, Harvey. 1988. Educating Reason: Rationality, Critical Thinking and Education, New York: Routledge. DOI: https://doi.org/10.4324/9781315001722

Strungariu, Maricela., Galița, Raluca., Bonta, Elena., Romedea, Adriana Gertruda. 2014. Reflections on language autobiographies/ Reflexions sur les autobiographies langagieres, Bacău: Alma Mater.

Uribe-Enciso, Olga.Licía, Uribe-Enciso, Diana.Sofía. & Daza, María del
    Pilar Vargas.2017. Critical thinking and its Importance in education:
    Some Reflections", Rastros Rostros, 19, N° 34: 78-88 – available at
    https://doi.org/10.16925/ra.v19i34.2144
Von Culin, Katherine.R., Tsukayama, Eli., Duckworth, Angela. L. 2014.
    "Unpacking grit: Motivational correlates of perseverance and passion
    for long-term goals", The Journal of Positive Psychology, 9, N° 4: 306-
    312. DOI: 10.1080/17439760.2014. 898320.
Watson, G. & Glaser, E. 2009. *Watson-Glaser Critical Thinking Appraisal
    Forms D and E*. San Antonio, TX: The Psychological Corporation.

CHAPTER 5

DEVELOPING HOST COMMUNICATION COMPETENCE IN STUDY ABROAD PROGRAMS. A STUDY OF TUNISIAN STUDENTS' AUTOBIOGRAPHIES OF INTERCULTURAL ENCOUNTERS

NADIA ABID & ASMA MOALLA

Introduction

Study abroad experience includes different challenges for students in trying to adapt to the new social and cultural milieu. The challenges students face in the new environment can be either enriching at academic, personal and social levels, or detrimental leading to failure, ethnocentrism and stereotyping (Jackson 2011; Meier and Daniels 2013). In SA, students develop their personalities academically, socially and interculturally through personal communication, that is, communication with the members of the host community, and mass communication through the direct contact with the cultural products of the host community such as mass media, arts etc. (Kim 2001).

As strangers (Kim 2001) in the new country and sojourners for varied periods of time, study abroad students go through a process of cross-cultural adaptation (Kim 2001) in which they feel stressed and confused, use adaptive strategies, and experience intercultural growth and identity change. Sojourners go through these stages at varying degrees depending on their personal predisposition and motivation for change and on environmental factors related to the host community such as the quality of interaction with, and acceptance of, the foreigner (Kim 2001). The success of the adaptation process, Kim (2001) argues, is enhanced by the development of Host Communication Competence (Henceforth, HCC) which means possessing the required and appropriate knowledge, attitudes and behaviors to operate successfully in the new environment. HCC is developed through trial and error and facing challenges during frequent contacts with the host community members.

The study of these encounters by means of different research methods such as narratives, autobiographies, interviews and scales has given insights into the processes and challenges that may enhance or hinder the sojourners'/students' adaptation. Researchers, for instance, reported significant growth of linguistic competence (Gao and Kennedy 2019), improvement of intercultural communication and adaptability skills (Rundstrom – Williams 2005), self-confidence and flexibility (Maharaja 2018), and higher intercultural sensitivity (Jackson 2011). Research based on Kim's model of HCC (2001) has shown that students' personality attributes, motivation, degree of openness and previous SA experiences have contributed to a higher degree of intercultural awareness, intercultural sensitivity and more confidence in communication (Jackson 2011; Sheldon 2010). Other studies focused on other factors affecting HCC such as the proximity between the students' culture and the host culture (Sheldon 2010), the influence of the host environment (Sobkowiak 2019) and the quality of interaction with the host environment (Meier and Daniels 2018; Sobkowiak 2019).

Previous literature on HCC in study abroad programs focused on the effects that the different factors, whether internal or external, have on students' development of HCC in general or in some of its components. Unlike the studies mentioned, this research examines the development of each of HCC's competences, and mainly focuses on the interaction among the different competences of HCC and their mutual influence in real intercultural contacts that SA students had with the members of the host community. The impact of personal factors and environmental factors are beyond the scope of this study. The focus is rather limited to the study of the mutual effect among competences. in real intercultural encounters. Studying the interrelationship among the three competences in action can lead to a deeper understanding of how one component has influenced the other to manage, or fail to manage, a situation of misunderstanding. To get that deeper understanding, a qualitative analysis of twelve Tunisian SA students' autobiographies of intercultural encounters (AIE) (Byram et al. 2009) was conducted following the AIE's guiding questions.

This study therefore seeks to investigate:

(1) the development of HCC among twelve Tunisian study abroad students in terms of three dimensions: cognitive, affective and operational

(2) the interrelatedness between the different components of the HCC.

1. Theoretical background

1.1. Study abroad and the development of intercultural skills

Study abroad programs such as Erasmus+, modern foreign language programs, and teaching assistant programs are recommended by high education institutions to develop students' academic, linguistic, professional and intercultural skills, and make them competitive on the global job market (Maharaja 2018). Intercultural skills in particular result from students' everyday contacts with the host community and are crucial for students' self-development, adaptation to the new culture, and success in international job settings (Deardorff 2006). Apart from academic achievement, study abroad is a context where students are immersed in a new culture, and during that immersion they face adaptive challenges while trying to make their ways in a new reality, form new attitudes, and subsequently become different persons (Kim 2001; Liddicoat and Scarino 2013).

Intercultural skills have equivalent models such as intercultural competence (Deardorff 2006), intercultural sensitivity (Bennett 2017), transcultural competence (Ting-Toomey 1999), and host communication competence (HCC) (Kim 2001). In study abroad programs, these models encompass competences that are developed during the students' process of managing the challenges they face in trying to adapt to the new cultural environment. Such a process, usually considered as a cross-cultural adaptation process (Kim 2001), is accompanied by feelings of stress, anxiety and confusion and may lead to change of mind, adoption of cultural practices, the ability to reconcile cultural differences, and the ability to manage stress (Kim 2001; Ting-Toomey 1999).

Kim's host communication competence (HCC) is a three-dimensional model that is composed of cognitive, affective and behavioral dimensions, which refer to the foreigner/sojourner's understanding of difference of intercultural communication norms, the willingness and motivation to manage stressful encounters, and the ability to use that understanding and motivation in actual intercultural contact situations. The intercultural experience lived during SA helps students develop intercultural skills and attitudes that enable them to behave appropriately and effectively in the new community, but also to better adapt to new cultural settings (Liddicoat and Scarino 2013). The development of such competences depends on the students' motivation to participate and engage in the intercultural experience offered by SA (Kim 2001; Liddicoat and Scarino 2013). Students' reaction and response to the challenges of living in the new environment largely depends on the strength of their identity (Mayer 2009), their ability to control feeling, and their openness to new experiences and change (Sheldon 2010).

Apart from its benefits for students, SA experience is reported to have negative outcomes. Students may not become more tolerant but more ethnocentric and less willing to participate in intercultural encounters (Jackson 2015). They may develop stereotypes rather than realistic views of the host cultural group. Students' ways and motivation to overcome those affective and cognitive and behavioral challenges can have an effect on their academic achievement, social experience, psychological well-being and day-to-day encounters in the host community (Mak and Kim 2011; Helpern et al. 2022).

1.2. Host communication competence

Crucial to the cross-cultural adaptation process is communication with the host community members and the development of host-communication competence (Kim 2001). Kim (2001) argues that the success of communication, and thus of adaptation, is conditioned by the individual's quantity and quality of communicative activities in the host environment that are marked by a process of "trial and error" (2001, 73). To overcome communication difficulties, the strangers' communication should be conducted in accordance with the natives' norms and values. Strangers (Kim's term for long-term and short-term sojourners) should develop Host-Communication Competence (2001, 98) to facilitate their cross-cultural adaptation process, a process that is influenced by the strangers' communication skills and environmental factors.

Host communication competence is made up of three interrelated key components which are not necessarily developed simultaneously. The development of one, however, does influence the development of the other. The three components or competences are: cognitive, affective, and operational.

1.2.1. The Cognitive Competence

The cognitive competence includes knowledge of the host communication system, cultural understanding, and cognitive complexity. Knowledge of the host communication system includes knowledge of language structure and language use, that is, knowledge and use of the verbal and non-verbal, of explicit and implicit language codes in the host language. Apart from this, individuals should have knowledge and understanding of the cultural milieu that provides contexts for specific situations. Cognitive competence also refers to understanding the cultural mindsets of the host community, which helps one better understand and interpret the natives' ways of thinking, behaving and communicating. Such understanding requires knowledge of cultural norms, values, beliefs, as well as knowledge of the host community's historical, political, religious, economic and educational institutions. Cognitive complexity is another component of the cognitive competence which comes as a result of a cumulative process of learning the host communication system and understanding the host culture. Cognitive complexity refers to the individuals' ability to identify similarities and differences between their original culture and the host culture and make more realistic and less stereotypical and simplistic interpretations of the host environment.

1.2.2. The Affective Competence

The affective competence comprises three main elements, which are adaptation motivation, identity flexibility, and aesthetic co-orientation. Kim argues that an increase in these components is accompanied by an increase in the success of cross-cultural adaptation. An individual can potentially successfully adapt to the host environment when they have high adaptation motivation. Adaptation motivation refers to the willingness to learn about and participate in the host environment. Identity flexibility refers to the willingness to accept the identity of the host culture, have positive and respectful attitudes towards the host culture and the original culture, and make changes in the original culture. The last component of the affective competence is aesthetic co-orientation. It refers to the willingness and ability to appreciate and participate in the aesthetic experiences of the natives, such as cultural productions, arts, music, sports etc.

1.2.3. The Operational Competence

Based on the assumption that strangers are better able to achieve social ease when they coordinate their behaviors with those of the natives, Kim (2001, 114) defines operational competence as "the ability to communicate and behave in accordance with the host cultural patterns." It is also the stranger's "capacity to select and enact behaviors that are likely to be effective and appropriate in various social situations." (2001, 117). This competence includes three main components: technical skills, synchrony, and resourcefulness. These components imply the strangers' ability to use language and enact behaviors that are suitable to the different social situations they participate in. Technical skills include the mastery of language skills, job skills, academic skills, and managing problematic social situations by using appropriate information from appropriate sources. Synchrony means using adjustment strategies, namely linguistic adjustment, to make speech intelligible. Synchrony refers to strangers' ability to achieve success and ease in social interaction by being able to coordinate their actions and behaviors with those of the natives and attain highly personalized psychological relationships with the natives. Resourcefulness means the ability to reconcile cultural differences, create plans to solve every problem using appropriate resources, manage intercultural encounters, and initiate and maintaining relationships.

Kim argues that enacting effective behaviors and communication is not only the outcome of the effective use of the operational competence but also the outcome of external circumstantial factors including the behavior of the other persons and the nature of the relationship involved.

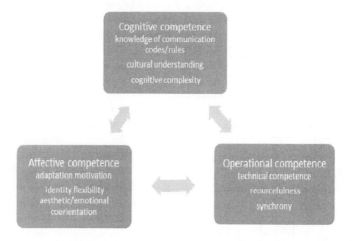

Figure 1: Interrelationship among the components of Host Communication Competence

1.3. Research on the development of HCC and Study Abroad

Research on the impact of SA on students' intercultural learning has focused on the development of language proficiency, personal growth, intercultural competence and HCC. The research has revealed that SA can have both positive and negative effects on the students' intercultural competence and HCC, and therefore on their cross-cultural adaptation.

In relation to intercultural communication, Rundson and Williams (2005) argued in their research that SA could result in the students' improvement of intercultural communication skills. The comparison between SA students and on-campus ones in terms of intercultural communication skills, namely intercultural adaptability and intercultural sensitivity, revealed a greater improvement and change in intercultural communication skills among SA students. Research has also shown that SA has a positive effect on other components of intercultural competence such as adaptability skills, language skills, stress management, and personal growth.

Based on her investigation of American students' development of intercultural competence as defined by Deardorff (2006), Maharaja (2018) asserted that the students' one-semester SA program enhanced their intercultural competence and personal development. They gained a deeper understanding of their own culture and the host culture, and thus became more self-confident, tolerant, assertive, and especially more flexible and willing to adapt to the differences of the new culture.

A study by Gao and Kennedy (2019) reported multiple positive effects of a short-term SA program performed by Chinese students. The results of the study showed the students' linguistic growth as well as the development on different aspects of intercultural competence such as increased knowledge of self and the other culture, intercultural communication skills, intercultural awareness, and positive attitudes. The results have highlighted the interrelatedness among linguistic, affective, cognitive and behavioral competences. Students, for instance, were found to be better able to accurately interpret people's behavior in the host culture and understand the reasons behind that behavior before jumping to conclusions and forming stereotypes. They developed language skills that enabled them to communicate better with the members of the host community. Language development together with flexibility and open-mindedness enabled students to use adaptive strategies and solve communication problems arising in emerging unfamiliar situations.

Similarly, based on Kim's (2001) definition of HCC and a scale based on that model, Sheldon (2010) found that international students on a SA program in the USA developed better HCC thanks to the high degree of their internal locus of control, i.e., the way they feel that the reward of their behavior is controlled by themselves and not by external factors. She asserted that the locus of control is the best explanation for/predictor of the students' host communication competence (the ability to communicate effectively in the host society). She added that the cultural proximity between the students' own culture and the host one, as well as the length of the duration of the stay had a positive impact on the participants' development of HCC.

In the Tunisian context, Abid and Moalla (2020) examined the extent to which 12 SA Tunisian students developed an intercultural identity by reflecting on intercultural encounters that marked their experience abroad. Findings were obtained from the analysis of their autobiographies of intercultural encounters based on Kim's (2001) stress-adaptation-growth dynamic taking into consideration the influence of personal attributes on intercultural identity construction. The findings revealed that the respondents experienced feelings of stress that triggered their choices of adaptive strategies, and that only a small number of them attained the growth stage.

In addition, the respondents' personal traits were found to have played a role in their identity development during the SA. Those who defined themselves as open-minded, curious and risk-taking were more successful in coping with stressful intercultural situations than those who identified themselves as sensitive and skeptical. The exploration of an intercultural encounter, unique as it was, has facilitated the tracing of the different stages that any sojourner can go through and has allowed the tracking of the process of identity development while trying to adapt to the new environment.

2. Methodology

2.1. Methods: The Autobiography of Intercultural Encounters (AIE)

The Autobiography of Intercultural Encounters (henceforth, AIE), the main data collection instrument used in this study, was initially an education tool designed by Byram et al. (2009) to help foreign language learners to reflect critically on their intercultural encounters (tense or pleasant) and their development of intercultural communicative competence (Byram, 1997; Barrett and Golubeva, 2022). The retrospective and reflective character of AIE enables learners to have a deeper understanding of the different cultural practices, behavioral and communication norms and attitudes which support their development of ICC. As Barrett and Golubeva (2022) argued, AIE was constructed for the purpose of assisting the development of ICC, which is why AIE incorporates all the dimensions of ICC, namely knowledge, attitudes, intercultural skills, intercultural awareness and action (Barrett and Golubeva, 2022).

AIE consists of questions that are sequenced and structured in a way that guides and scaffolds respondents' thinking and reflection on the encounter they had with a culturally different person. The questions proceed from simple questions about their names, their description of themselves and narration of the encounter to more complex ones about their feelings, reactions and the reaction of their interlocutors. The AIE ends with a question on subsequent action(s) taken or to be taken as a consequence of the encounter.

The problematic intercultural encounter that participants report can be an instance of the adaptive challenges that foreigners, and study abroad students in particular, face in their process of adapting to the new social and cultural environment. In this respect, Kim (2001, 6) states: "Each adaptive challenge, in turn, offers them an opportunity to grow beyond the perimeters of the original culture." Just like ICC, HCC is not only the outcome of interpersonal (Kim, 2001) or intercultural encounters (Byram, 1997) but also a prerequisite for successful and effective intercultural communication with members of the host community. Kim (2001) adds that intercultural encounters within the host community offer strangers opportunities to evaluate and validate their behaviors and the natives'

Given the similarities between the components of ICC and HCC and the importance of intercultural encounters for their development, the current study finds it relevant to use the AIE as a data collection instrument to collect information about a marking encounter in a SA students' experience in the host environment. Although the purposes and periods of residence abroad differ from immigrants to students, both of them go through a complex process of adaptation that requires affective, cognitive and behavioral skills, that is HCC (Kim, 2001) or ICC (Byram, 1997).

2.2. Analytical framework: Host Communication Competence

TABLE 1: Host communication competence

Cognitive competence	Affective competence	Operational competence
Knowledge of the host communication system: knowledge of language, verbal and non-verbal codes, language use	Adaptation motivation: -willingness to participate in the host environment -willingness to learn about the host environment	Technical skills: Language skills Job skills Problem solving skills Academic skills
Cultural understanding: knowledge and understanding of the host culture norms, beliefs, attitudes, and institutions	Identity flexibility: -willingness to accept and respect the identity of the other culture - willingness to make changes in the original culture -have positive attitudes towards one's identity and others'	Synchrony: Making adjustments
Cognitive complexity: ability to differentiate between the culture of origin and host culture/ ability to make realistic interpretation of the target culture	Aesthetic co-orientation: -willingness and ability to participate in the aesthetic experience of the natives	Resourcefulness: -Reconcile cultural differences and make plans -Seek and use appropriate resources to solve problems -Manage face-to-face interactions -Initiating and maintaining relationships

2.3. Participants

The participants in this study are twelve Tunisian English graduate students who participated in study abroad programs of different durations and in different English- and French speaking countries. The duration of their stays ranged from six months to four years. Their intercultural encounters took place in different places such as host families, student accommodation, and public places such as church, cafés, and a bank. The participants were students in the English department at the Faculty of Arts and Humanities of Sfax, Tunisia, who went on study abroad by individual initiatives and in the form of exchange programs organized by the American embassy in Tunisia. The table below summarizes the participants' profiles: their host countries, the stay duration, and the place of the intercultural encounter they chose for the study.

TABLE 2: Participants

Participant	Host country	Duration of stay	Place of the encounter
AIE 1	USA	One year	Church
AIE 2	USA	9 months	Students' dorm
AIE 3	USA	Almost one year	Host family's place
AIE 4	USA	16 months	Hostel
AIE 5	UK	7 years	Student accommodation
AIE 6	UK	13 months	Student accommodation
AIE 7	Sweden	6 months	Language café
AIE 8	France	6 years	Host family
AIE 9	Belgium	4 years	university
AIE 10	USA	Almost one year	Host family's place
AIE 11	UK	One year	Bank
AIE 12	France	10 years	A conference

2.4. Procedures

The autobiographies of intercultural encounters were collected from the 12 Tunisian SA students mentioned above and analyzed by tracking their development of HCC's components, namely the cognitive, affective and operational competences. The AIEs were quantitatively analyzed by extracting and classifying utterances according to the type of competence and instances of interrelatedness. The qualitative analysis was conducted on utterances reflecting each type of competence, and on those where competences affect one another in the encounters.

The utterances were mainly extracted from the second section of the AIEs where respondents were asked to reflect on and evaluate their experiences by indicating their feelings, reactions, the change they experienced after the encounter and their future behavior. The answers were analyzed by identifying the type of the competence developed (cognitive, affective, and operational) as a result of the encounter.

The first part of the AIE provided a detailed description of the encounter, the participants, their emotions and reactions during the encounter. This first part helped in identifying and understanding the types of misunderstanding, the participants' thoughts, emotions and reactions.

3. Findings

This section identifies and explains the HCC's cognitive, affective and operational dimensions. This study is based on the assumption that students' development of HCC is determined by their ability to understand differences in communication norms, their motivation to manage stressful intercultural encounters, and their ability to use both knowledge and motivation to cope with actual contact situations. To give an overall view of the participants' development of HCC, the frequency distribution of the three dimensions is calculated. Table 3 shows that there is an overwhelming presence of statements referring to the operational dimension; whereas statements referring to the cognitive and affective dimensions are evenly distributed.

The even distribution of the cognitive and affective competences shows a balance in the development of both competences, which indicates their interrelationship. Participants' development of operational competence is conditioned, according to Kim (2001), by the degree of their development of cognitive competence (knowledge of intercultural communication norms) and affective competence (motivation to adapt). The table shows that the balance in the distribution of both affective and cognitive competences has led to a remarkable development of the operational/behavioral competence.

TABLE 3: The frequency distribution of the three dimensions across the autobiographies

Dimension	Frequency
Cognitive	15
Affective	14
Operational	44
Total	73

The table shows that the balance in the distribution of both affective and cognitive competences has led to a remarkable development of the operational/behavioral competence. Table 4 summarizes the distribution of the three dimensions in each autobiography to understand the way the development of cognitive and affective competences operationalizes in successful appropriate behaviors within the host community.

TABLE 4: The distribution of HCC's three competences in each autobiography

	1	2	3	4	5	6	7	8	9	10	11	12	Total
Cognitive	0	2	1	1	1	3	1	1	0	2	2	1	15
Affective	3	0	3	2	2	1	0	1	0	0	2	0	14
Operational	1	5	4	2	4	4	3	4	3	5	3	6	44

The frequency distribution of the three dimensions (competences) provided an overview of the general tendency of the participants' HCC. The qualitative analysis based on selected statements from the participants' autobiographies offers insights into, first, the development of each competence, and second, the interrelatedness between the three competences.

3.1. The cognitive competence

The cognitive competence refers to the participants' development of knowledge of the host communication codes/rules, cultural understanding, and cognitive complexity. Participants' statements revealed development of knowledge of the host communication systems, cultural understanding, and cognitive complexity. Three experiences were selected for analysis, namely autobiography 2, 10 and 11.

Example one:
Participant 11, an MA male student in Sunderland, was greeted by a bank teller by 'Hi flower'. He was surprised and intrigued because in his own culture addressing a man by 'a flower' is inappropriate.

When he was greeted by means of the word "flower", participant 11 felt surprised and intrigued as he thought that this form was an inappropriate way to greet males. His lack of knowledge of the cultural norms of greeting in the host community led to feelings of surprise. The experience, however, was enriching as it added to his knowledge about the norms of greeting in the host culture and led him to compare and find out similar ways and expressions in his own culture. He stated: "when thinking about the experience, I could think of similar expressions in Tunisian Arabic that we Tunisians seem to take for granted," and added: "I drew the conclusion that despite the differences in culture, we seem to share a lot more than we think we do."

Example two:

Participant 2 is a female exchange student in the USA whose roommate's father cracked racist jokes about Arabs. She chose not to take it personally and she tried to find an explanation for his behavior instead.

The second example shows that the participant has developed cognitive complexity by being able to make a realistic interpretation of the joke/behavior of her American friend's father who made racist jokes about Arabs whenever he met her. She interpreted his behavior as a lack of intercultural communication skills and not as an act of racism. Her background knowledge of the man's history obtained from her friend led her to make that interpretation. She said (AIE 2): "I chose to go with the idea that he has a 'funky' sense of humor and he somewhat lacks in the area of communication."

She managed to overcome the embarrassing situation thanks to the knowledge she had about different cultures. She explained: "I faked a shocked face and laughed spontaneously because the joke was funny, from a western perspective, which I understood very clearly"

Example three:

In this example, participant 10, a female MA student in the USA, behaved inappropriately by hanging her jacket on the Cross in her room. Her religious host sister felt offended and moved the participant to another room after having a discussion about the incident.

During the discussion, AIE 10 realized that the act which she considered funny was perceived as inconsiderate and disrespectful by the host family. The discussion made her understand that the presence of Jesus Christ was important for them and that covering his head prevented the family from God's protection. She also realized that the sacred is different from one culture to another. She ended up relativizing her point of view due to the new information she got about the host culture norms and values. She developed a kind of cultural understanding that helped her modify her attitudes and behavior. She stated: "it made me reflect on many issues and values that are so normal and ethical in my vintage point but could be perceived differently by the other."

3.2. The affective competence

The participants' autobiographies have demonstrated traces of affective competence reflected in their willingness to accept and respect the identity of other cultures, to learn about the host environment, and in their positive attitudes towards their own and the other culture.

- *Positive attitudes towards the identity of one's own and the other's culture*

Although intercultural encounters could be challenging and tense, especially when dealing with sensitive controversial issues such as religion, they could have positive effects on the participants' attitudes towards the host environment. For instance, participant 3 had a discussion with her host sister about the different stories of Mary (Mother of Jesus) in Islam (her religion) and Christianity (her host's religion). The tension participant 3 experienced in discussing Islam's attitudes towards Mary's story (giving birth to Jesus Christ while being a virgin) and some Christians' hostile attitudes towards Muslims led to better understanding and a more successful relationship with the host family. She mentioned that the difference made their relationship closer rather than distant and confrontational. She stated: "the situation has made me closer to my (host) family and I started appreciating the efforts they are making to make me feel more like home," and added: "I also felt that we are emotionally connected in spite of the cultural and religious differences."

- *Willingness to accept and respect the identity of the other culture*

Willingness to accept and respect the identity of the other culture is another affective skill that some participants developed. They admitted that they had become more open-minded, tolerant and flexible. Participant 3, who had a tense discussion about religion with her host sister, asserted: "now, I have become more open-minded and tolerant towards differences and I do not make firm claims about religion." Relativized attitudes are also another sign of developing affective competence. Intercultural encounters taught participants to accept the identity of the others without making generalizations or judging the others from their own perspectives. For instance, participant 4, who had a tense discussion with her Israeli and American roommates over the Israeli-Palestinian conflict, ended up accepting her interlocutors' perspectives and relativizing her own. She claimed: "my opinion about the conflict did not change, but I will not put everyone in the same basket."

- *Willingness to learn about the host environment*

The intercultural encounters increased the participants' curiosity about knowing and discovering other cultures. Participant 5 is an MA student in the UK who had the chance to attend a party with international students and was impressed by the cultural diversity. She mentioned: "I enjoyed my time learning about cultures and experiences totally different to mine." Opening up to people from different cultures and exchanging views on sensitive topics is another indication of the participants' willingness to learn about the other. Participant 3, for example, stated: "I really enjoy opening up to other people and sharing experiences with them".

3.3. The operational competence

In reference to table (2) the findings demonstrated that the operational competence is highly developed in the participants compared with the affective and cognitive competences. The intercultural encounters that participants took part in had different impacts on the way they behaved in subsequent encounters. They acquired language and problem solving skills, they learned how to use affective and cognitive resources to solve communication problems, how to adjust their behavior and language to manage threatening and stressful situations, and how to initiate and maintain relationships with people from the host community. Few of them, however, did not show intention to adjust when faced with a disturbing situation. The findings obtained from the analysis of the operational competence are described in detail on the basis of its sub-components: technical skills, synchrony, and resourcefulness.

- *Technical skills*

In terms of technical skills, participant 7 stressed the importance of language cafés organized by the host university in Sweden which brought together people from different cultures to learn language and culture. She managed to learn the host community's language and that facilitated her interactions and relationship building. She mentioned: "I thought about organizing a language café when going back. The experience gave me access to various language skills and allowed me to know many people who I am still friend with till now." For participant 9, knowledge of language was problematic and triggered her mentor's racist attitude. Instead of being a facilitating tool for communication and integration, her mastery and use of the language was rejected by a Dutch-speaking Belgian mentor.

- *Synchrony: making adjustments*

Making adjustments is one way of adapting to the host community's norms of communication and behavior and facilitating communication. Findings from the analysis of the participants' autobiographies revealed three types of adjustments: adjustment of thoughts and feelings, linguistic adjustment, and adjustment of behavior. Participant 3, for instance, learned to adjust her thoughts on religion to relativize her view of everything, including religion. She mentioned: "we adjusted our thoughts and dogmatic feelings about religion and we accepted the proposition that there is nothing as totally correct or wrong even in religion." She added that the adjustments of thoughts and making them fit with the other's had a positive effect on her feelings, attitudes and relationships. She stated: "I also felt that we are emotionally connected in spite of the cultural and religious differences."

Another example illustrating how language mastery helped the participants' integration is provided by participant 6 who lived in student accommodation in Yorkshire with British students having no idea about Tunisia. She spoke English with a different accent, which made her look like an alien. The reaction of her British mates to her accent and nationality led her to make efforts to adjust her accent to theirs so that she could be more intelligible and more accepted. Participant 6 stated: "I kept asking my housemates in private about certain words and expressions and their appropriate use. I kept them in mind and then kept rehearsing them every night in my room in the same accent and tone."

The same participant reported learning to adjust her behavior so that it became suitable to that of the host environment. She made efforts to participate in everyday social activities to understand how Yorkshire people think and behave. She said: "I kept going up with them and watching their favorite TV shows and we shared food all the time and I seized every occasion to chat with them about any single topic just to learn about the Yorkshire mentality." Another example of adjusting one's behavior to the host community is presented by participant 11 who did not appreciate the bank teller's greeting him by "Hi flower", a greeting expression that is not appreciated by men in his own culture. Understanding that cultural difference made him adjust his way of greeting. He embraced that form of greeting and used it with the members of the host community (Sunderland, UK). He stated: "The experience changed me in the sense of embracing these forms of greetings," and added "through my stay, I ended up using these forms of greetings often with the local shopkeepers, grocery store employees and it felt natural."

- *Resourcefulness*

Managing face -to-face interactions

Face -to-face interactions are stressful and challenging situations where strangers have to cope with stress and confusion emerging out of ambiguity. In this study, intercultural encounters put affective and cognitive pressure on the participants and they had to use their cognitive resources and flexibility to communicate effectively with the natives of the host community. The participants mentioned that they learned from the encounters strategies that helped and would help them communicate successfully with people of different cultural backgrounds. Some reported suppressing feelings of anger and surprise as an avoidance strategy so that communication should go smoothly when they faced disturbing situations or attitudes. They learned the necessity of keeping calm and being positive before they started looking for explanations of the natives' behavior. Participant 2 mentioned: "I suppressed any feelings of upsetness and I pretended to be OK with it." Along with respecting people's differences, opening to others, listening to them, and trying to understand their reasons are strategies the participants used to manage face-to-face interactions. Participant 10, whose behavior was perceived as inappropriate and offensive by her host sister, admitted that she should have taken the issue more seriously: "I also feel that I should not have just apologized and made her feel that it was just a simple act. I should have gone to her and listened to her in a more respectful way."

Using appropriate resources to solve problems

Managing misunderstanding required the participants' use of knowledge of the host community's norms of communication and behavior so that they could communicate with the members of the host community and establish bonds with them. The intercultural experiences they had taught them to evaluate the reasons for the other's behavior and not jump to conclusions and prejudices. Participant 2 mentioned: "I am rather encouraging evaluating situations before jumping to conclusions and making strong reactions that could be avoided by a simple gesture or a subtle expression." They also learned to control their emotions of anger, surprise and confusion and to tried to understand the situation instead of preventing confrontation and tension. The same participant stated: "In a multicultural setting, confrontation and making sure you correct people at every turn are not the healthy option to opt for." It is also reported that willingness to discuss and negotiate the issue of misunderstanding is the key to not only manage misunderstanding in communication but also to establish strong bonds with host culture members. As illustration to this finding, participant 3 reported: "I started believing in the power of negotiating differences and discussing serious issues; and if we manage to discuss them and still maintain our relationships, a stronger bond can be established."

Informed problem solving, especially communication misunderstanding, is another behavioral/operational skill that the participants developed. Participants reported that they had learned from the encounters they narrated, that knowledge of the other's norms is important for effective communication, relativized views and rational judgements. Participant 4, for instance, mentioned that the encounter with the Israeli and American roommates and the discussion they had over the Israeli-Palestinian conflict, despite being tense, led her to do research on the history of the conflict to better understand her Israeli roommate's perspective. Doing research to get knowledge of the problem is the outcome of the tense conversation, which she thought led to a more relativized view. She mentioned: "The conversation led me to do more research on the history of the region and how things have escalated," and concluded that: "Each individual has his or her own story and I should listen to that first before judging them."

Doing research on culture does not only encompass the host culture but also the participant's. A better and more comprehensive knowledge of one's own cultural norms and practices can make oneself better understood by the other in communication, especially if that culture is unknown to the other. The intercultural encounter was an opportunity for participant 6 to do research on her culture to give answers to her interlocutors' questions. Knowledge of her culture made her able to define who she was and be more accepted by her mates. The communication became smoother as her mates became more knowledgeable of the new culture and they no longer treated her as an alien. Participant 6 mentioned: "I have done a lot of research about stuff related to Tunisia, religion, geography, culture, history, people etc. because they kept asking me a lot of questions and I looked like an idiot as I did not know how to answer half of the questions."

Reconciling cultural differences
Another behavioral/operational skill that is necessary for host communication is the ability to reconcile cultural differences. The participants reported that they became more aware and respectful of cultural differences. They learned to be careful when interacting with people from another culture in order not to offend them and /be offended. Participant 10 realized the importance of considering other people's differences before and while

interacting with the others. She asserted: "I became more careful about my behavior; more attentive to things that matter a lot to them and try to have their cultural differences in mind before I react or say anything." She added: "I started paying attention to details about their culture in order not to offend anyone."

Along with awareness of differences, trying to explain the cultural underpinnings of those differences to the interlocutor is a reconciling strategy that gives meaning and logic to what is different and, therefore, bridges the gap between the participants' culture and the host culture.

Participant 12, for example, lived in the UK for a while and was invited to a movie projection with internationals. She paid for the ticket of her Turkish mate who reacted to her behavior in an aggressive way instead of thanking her. In reflecting on her encounter, participant 12 reported a change in her behavior. She mentioned that explaining the cultural difference underlying her behavior could have solved the misunderstanding that happened when she paid for her Turkish mate's ticket. She reported: "I should explain that in our culture, paying for someone's sandwich, drink or cinema ticket when together is an act of generosity." She added that: "since then, I have become careful about my behavior when I am with someone from a different culture."

For some participants, the encounters triggered their willingness to initiate new encounters, meet new people, and maintain friendly relationships either with host families or other students. An illustration of this is given by participants 1 who stated: "I experienced even more interesting encounters and adventures after that day." The effect was even more positive with participant five whose encounter led her to travel and meet people. She said: "this experience strengthened my will to keep travelling and meeting new people. I stayed in the UK, kept in touch with most of my international friends and of course I enjoyed explaining the difference between standard Arabic and the various dialects in the Arab world."

3.4. Interrelationship between cognitive, affective, and operational competences

In the absence, and impossibility, of a longitudinal study, the AIE given its reflective, retrospective and future-oriented nature, can provide insights on the development of HCC in the light of a particular incident. AIE can give an idea about past events, present readings of the event, and future actions to take, which can be useful in tracking the participants' development of cognitive, affective and operational competences. The analysis of the interaction among the three competences in intercultural encounters is done based on a selection of four AIEs, namely AIE 6, 10, 11 and 9.

AIE 6

Participant 6 lived with four English girls in a student accommodation in York where there were few Arabs and no Tunisians. The student was treated as alien by her mates because her physical appearance and language did not match the stereotypical image they had about Arabs, Muslims and Africans. They kept asking her why she looked different and how she was able to speak English. To correct the stereotypes and make herself understood and accepted, she made efforts to learn their accent and to look for more information about her country to answer they queries. Her lack of knowledge of her country and culture led her to do research and adjust her accent to be in synchrony with the host environment's language variety. She stressed the importance of knowledge to adapt to any society different from one's own. She reported: "You need to know about the place you are going to before going there." After the encounter and doing research, she became more knowledgeable: "I am more knowledgeable and can discuss any topic freely."

Her affective competence did not result from her knowledge of the country. The stress she felt when interacting with the British girls led her to make efforts to know their language, which helped her communicate effectively with them. She also made efforts to know their mentality by participating in their social activities. This made her behave appropriately and made her behavior and her culture appreciated and accepted by others. She said: "I am so happy and proud that I succeeded in showing these people how amazing our country, religion, and culture are."

AIE 10

Participant 10 lived with a religious American family. She had a serious discussion about religious beliefs and she was moved to another room because she hang her jacket on Jesus Christ's head. Participant 10 thought that the host family overreacted and that her behavior was normal. After the discussion she acquired knowledge about the value of having Jesus Christ in a Christian Byzantine house. Covering Jesus' head removes security and blessing from the family. The knowledge the participant acquired about the importance of religion for the family and the value of Jesus Christ for them made her change her point of view, and thus she became more tolerant and open-minded: "It made me reflect on many issues and values that are so normal and ethical from my vantage point but could be perceived differently by others."

Knowledge of the importance of Jesus Christ for the security of the family and the value he had for the family led her to recognize the cultural differences and behave in a more reasonable way to solve the problem. Being aware of the importance of listening to people in a respectful way was a good behavior that led to a friendlier relationship. This conclusion explains how solving the problem by listening should be accompanied by respect of cultural differences, which is an affective variable. This is an example of the simultaneous functioning of the two competences. Another example of the simultaneous operation of the three competences is the use of knowledge for better behavior. The participant mentioned that knowledge of the culture coupled with a careful and considerate behavior led to a better communication and relation. She said: "I became more careful about my behavior, more attentive to things that matter a lot to them, and tried to have their cultural differences in mind before I reacted or said anything." An example that combines the cognitive and affective competences is her improvement of her knowledge of the host culture in order not to offend its people: "I started paying attention to details about their culture in order not to offend them."

AIE 11
Due to the lack of knowledge of the way people greet one another in Sunderland, participant 11 did not appreciate the bank teller's way of greeting him, which he thought was not acceptable with men in his own culture. Thinking about the event after it ended, he started reflecting on similar expressions and ways of greeting in Arabic, his mother tongue. The encounter enriched his knowledge of his mother tongue as he learned about ways of greeting in his own culture that also used metaphorical expressions. He said: "I drew the conclusion that despite the differences in culture, we seem to share a lot more than we think we do." The new acquired knowledge triggered attitudes of tolerance and flexibility: "It changed me in the sense of being more open to accept cultural differences," and his willingness to adjust his language use to the norms of the host community by embracing such kind of greeting. He mentioned: "I ended up using these forms of greetings often with the local shopkeeper, grocery store employees and it felt natural."

AIE 9
Not all encounters yielded positive outcomes in terms of the development of the HCC. Participant 9 is a medical student who learned the Dutch language, one of the official languages in his new country of residence, Belgium, in order to study and work. Having mastered the language, she

started using it with a Belgian colleague. The experience was not pleasant as the colleague she talked to did not accept her speaking Dutch, his language, and made a racist remark. The participants' answers showed no traces of developing cognitive competence but implicit affective competences. The autobiography revealed a limited variety of behavioral skills. The participant, despite being disturbed by her colleague's racist reaction, considered his behavior as an isolated instance and she insisted on continuing to speak the language in subsequent encounters. She did not give importance to the incident or to the person, and behaved as if nothing had happened. Her behavior may imply her strong willingness and determination to participate in the host environment and succeed in her job and life in Belgium. She reported: "I continued speaking his language. I behaved as if nothing happened. She added: "he has to evaluate his behavior. It is his own problem, not mine…. You have to make progress, make your own way and learn to be strong." This is a clear example of how the affective competence helped the development of the operational one.

4. Discussion

The findings obtained from the qualitative analysis are discussed following the two major foci of this research, namely the role of SA in developing Tunisian students HCC, and the interrelatedness of the three components of HCC during the process of HCC development.

The role of SA in the Tunisian Students' Development of HCC

The findings revealed that all dimensions of HCC were developed, with an overwhelming presence of the operational dimension (cognitive 14, Affective 15, Operational 47). In terms of cognitive competence, Tunisian students showed signs of developing knowledge and understanding of the host communities' communication norms and patterns and an ability to make realistic interpretations of the intercultural situations they experienced. They were also able to discover and understand their own culture through communication with the other. This finding was confirmed by Gao and Kennedy (2019) who concluded that SA, despite being a short-term one, influenced Chinese students' awareness of self and other.

In terms of affective competence, the respondents expressed positive attitudes towards the other's culture and identity. They became more open-minded and tolerant and developed more relativized attitudes towards differences. These findings are in line with Maharaja's (2018) findings which emphasized the positive impact of SA on American students' personal growth. Similar to our findings, the study highlighted the importance of SA in promoting students' self-confidence, tolerance, flexibility, and willingness to adapt to the differences of the host culture. In a different context, Gao and Kennedy's study (2019) revealed how short-term SA program positively influenced Chinese students' attitudes towards the American culture they experienced in Texas.

As far as the operational competence is concerned, the participants developed linguistic skills. They became more proficient and adapted their language to that of the native speakers. Gao and Kennedy's (2019) research showed that Chinese students in the USA developed different operational skills such as language skills and ability to use their knowledge of the host-culture and language to solve communication problems. They showed ability to adjust their behaviors to the host community's norms, manage stressful encounters, initiate interactions, and maintain relationships with the members of the host community. Similar results indicated the development of intercultural communication skills (Rundson-Williams 2005), and linguistic growth and behavioral competence (Gao and Kennedy 2019).

The interrelatedness of the three components in the developmental process
Table (1) shows that the cognitive and affective competences are evenly distributed and that the operational competence is more frequent. According to Kim's (2001) theory of cross-cultural adaptation and HCC model, the development of operational competence is conditioned by the development of the affective and cognitive ones. Based on that assumption and the findings in table (1), it can be concluded that the three components are interrelated and that the affective and cognitive competences have led to the development of the operational competence (being higher in frequency than the others). This finding is in line with Kim's (2001) claim that the three components of HCC are interrelated and interactive, which facilitates their participation and intercultural transformation within the host society. Kim also argues that sojourners with a high degree of cognitive competence, i.e., knowledge of the host community's codes of communication and behavior and understanding of cultural aspects and practices, are more willing to adapt and communicate with the natives, and more open and flexible towards difference. The sojourners possessing such kind of knowledge and attitudes are more likely to interact effectively and appropriately in the host environment.

The qualitative analysis of the Tunisian students' AIEs showed examples where the cognitive competence affected the affective and operational competences. In fact, knowledge of the host culture and its norms resulted in successful adaptation strategies as well as tolerance of difference and respect for other ways of behaving and thinking. Lack of knowledge has been mentioned as a reason for misunderstanding, miscommunication and feelings of stress and anxiety.

In some examples, the ability to adjust one's behavior and language to those of the host community enabled the participants to know more about it and develop more relativized attitudes towards the community and the world cultures as a whole. The relationship between the different components of HCC is confirmed by Gao and Kennedy's research (2019) which found a strong interrelatedness between linguistic, affective, cognitive and behavioral competences. The interrelatedness of the cognitive and affective competences appeared in the participants' ability to make the right interpretation of the reality and avoid wrong judgment. The linguistic competence, which is a component of the operational competence (Kim 2001), along with the participants' open-mindedness and flexibility led them to use adaptive strategies and solve emerging communication problems.

Conclusion

Given the importance of HCC in cross cultural adaptation, the present study investigated the role of SA programs in promoting Tunisian students' HCC. Twelve Tunisian SA students were asked to write guided AIEs in which they reported and reflected on an intercultural encounter from which they learned about the other and themselves. The qualitative analysis of the AIEs focused on the development of the three components of HCC as well as the interrelatedness of those components during the students' process of cross-cultural adaptation. The findings of the quantitative analysis revealed the development of the three competences, with the operational competence as the most developed one. In fact, the students have been shown to develop positive, flexible, respectful, and relativized attitudes towards the host community's members' culture(s) and identities. They also gained knowledge of the host community's norms of behavior and communication, acquired linguistic competence, and developed the skill of managing challenging encounters and solving communication problems.

The interrelatedness between the three components was reflected in the students' ability to manage miscommunication through the adoption of flexible attitudes and to use their knowledge of the host environment's culture to communicate effectively in intercultural interactions. No negative outcome was tracked in the AIEs, which might be due to the limited number of participants and their mastery of the English language, given that all of them were majoring in English. A study with a larger sample of participants who have different language proficiency levels may yield different results.

This study has different implications for Tunisian universities intending to go international by engaging in designing SA programs and exchanges. Given the increasing number of Tunisian students going on SA programs, more importance should be given to incorporating intercultural communication courses in the curriculum which provide guided critical reflection on lived or imagined intercultural encounters as a preparation for future study abroad sojourns. For the international experience to be beneficial to students' integration and academic success, teaching/learning activities in intercultural communication courses should be more oriented towards interaction, self-reflection, and self-analysis. Teaching and assessment tools such as AIEs, narratives and diaries can be helpful to both teachers and students in keeping track of their emotional, cognitive and behavioral changes during their intercultural experience. In addition, it can give teachers and students an idea of the cognitive, affective and behavioral areas that should be improved to increase the students' chances of success in the new environment they intend to live and study in.

References

Abid, Nadia Moalla, Asma. 2020. Tunisian Students' Intercultural Identity Development in Study Abroad. I-LanD Journal 1:151-173.
DOI: 10.26379/IL2018001_12

Barret, Martyn and Irina Golubeva. 2022. "From Intercultural Communicative Competence to Intercultural Citizenship: Preparing Young People for Citizenship in a Culturally Diverse Democratic World." In Intercultural Learning in Language Education and Beyond: Evolving Concepts, Perspectives and Practices, edited by Troy McConachy, Irina Golubeva and Manuela Wagner, 60-83. Bristol: Multilingual Matters.

Bennett, Milton J. 2017. "Development Model of Intercultural Sensitivity." In International Encyclopedia of Intercultural Communication, edited by Young Yun Kim. Wiley-Blackwell.
http://dx.doi.org/10.1002/9781118783665.ieicc0182

Byram, Michael. 1997. Teaching and Assessing Intercultural Communicative Competence. Clevedon: Multilingual Matters.

Byram, Michael., Martyn Barret, Julia Ipgrave, Robert Jackson, and Maria DC. Méndez-García. 2009. Autobiography of Intercultural Encounters. Context, concepts and theories. Strasbourg: Council of Europe.

Council of Europe. 2018. Common European Framework of Reference for Languages: Learning, Teaching, Assessment – Companion volume with new descriptors. Strasbourg: Council of Europe.
https://rm.coe.int/cefr-companion-volume-with-new-descriptors-2018/1680787989

Deardorff, Darla.K. 2006. "Identification and Assessment of Intercultural Competence as a Student Outcome of Internationalization." Journal of Studies in International Education 10, No.3: 241-266.
https://doi.org/10.1177/1028315306287002

Dypedahl, Magne. 2022. "Exploring the Systematic Use of Intercultural Encounters in the English Classroom." In Moving English Language Teaching Forward, edited by Magne Dypedahl, 91–115. Oslo: Cappelen Damm Akademisk.
https://doi.org/10.23865/noasp.166.ch5

Gao, Shuangmei, and Teresa Kennedy, T.J. 2019. "Intercultural Competence Development of Chinese Students After a Short-Term Study Abroad Experience." Sino-US English Teaching 16, No. 5: 177-196 doi:10.17265/1539-8072/2019.05.001.

Halpern, Clarisse, Bruno Halpern, and Hasan Aydin. 2022. "International Students' Lived Experiences with Intercultural Competence in a Southwest Florida University." International Journal of Multicultural Education 24, No.1: 47- 67.
http://dx.doi.org/10.18251/ijme.v24i1.3013

Jackson, Jane. 2005. "Assessing Intercultural Learning through Introspective Accounts." Frontiers: The Interdisciplinary Journal of Study Abroad 11, No. 1: 165-186.
http://dx.doi.org/10.36366/frontiers.v11i1.156

Jackson, Jane. 2009. "Intercultural Learning on Short-Term Sojourns." Intercultural education 20, No. 1: 59-71.
http://dx.doi.org/10.1080/14675980903370870

Jackson, J. 2011. "Host language proficiency, Intercultural Sensitivity, and Study Abroad." Frontiers: The Interdisciplinary Journal of Study Abroad 21, No. 1: 167-188.

Jackson, Jane. 2013. "The Transformation of "a frog in the well". A path to a more Intercultural, Global Mindset." In Social and cultural aspects of language learning in study abroad, edited by Celeste Kinginger, 179-204. Amsterdam/Philadephia: John Benjamins Publishing Company.

Jackson, Jane. 2015. "Becoming Interculturally Competent: Theory to Practice in International Education." International Journal of Intercultural Relations 48: 91-107.
https://doi.org/10.1016/j.ijintrel.2015.03.012

Kim, Young Y. 2001. Becoming Intercultural: An Integrative Theory of Communication and Cross-Cultural Adaptation. London: SAGE Publications, Inc.

Liddicoat, Anthony J. and Angela Scarino. 2013. Intercultural language teaching and learning. West-Sussex: Wiley-Blackwell

Meier, Gabriela. and Harry Daniels. 2013. "'Just Not Being Able to Make Friends': Social Interaction During Year Abroad in Modern Foreign Language Degrees." Research Papers in Education 28, No. 2: 212-238. http://dx.doi.org/10.1080/02671522.2011.629734

Maharaja, Gita. 2018. "The Impact of Study Abroad on College Students' Intercultural Competence and Personal Development." Research and Review: Journal of Phi Beta Delta Honor Society for International Scholars 7, No. 2: 18-41. Available at: https://eric.ed.gov/?id=EJ1188735

Mak, Anita S., and In Kuk Kim. 2011. "Korean International Students' Coping Resources and Psychological Adjustment in Australia." The Journal of Multicultural Society 2, No.1: 56-84.

Mayer, Claude-Hélène.2009. "Managing Conflicts through Strength of Identity." Management revue-Socio-Economic Studies 20, No.3: 268-293. DOI 10.1688/1861-9908_mrev_2009-03_Mayer

Rundstrom -Willimas, Tracy. 2005. "Exploring the Impact of Study Abroad on Students' Intercultural Communication Skills: Adaptability and Sensitivity." Journal of Studies in International Education 9, No. 4: 356- 371.

Sheldon, Pavica. 2010. "Host Communication Competence and the Locus of Control of International Students in the USA." Journal of intercultural communication, 24. Available at: https://immi.se/oldwebsite/nr24/sheldon.htm

Sobkowiak, Pawel. 2019. "The Impact of Studying Abroad on Students' Intercultural Competence: An Interview Study." Studies in Second Language Teaching and Learning Vol9, N°.4: 681-710. http://dx.doi.org/10.14746/ssllt.2019.9.4.6

Ting-Toomey, Stella.1999. Communicating across Cultures. New York: The Guilford Press.

CHAPTER 6

INTERCULTURALITY AS THE OUTCOME OF RELIGIOUS CULTURAL ENCOUNTERS IN THE *AUTOBIOGRAPHY OF MALCOLM X*

SADOK DAMAK

Introduction

The intercultural phenomenon offers a field of great interest to researchers in social psychology whose concern is the mutation of identities. In this respect, the study undertaken for this paper looks for the way cultural changes articulate so that they produce new identity vehicles. To this end, it investigates the primary data provided by the *Autobiography of Malcolm X*. The author of this book was a well-known figure, outspokenly giving an additional voice to the 1950s and 1960s African American militant activism. Malcolm X publicly substituted his hesitant Christian faith with the Islamic one. Indeed, he embraced—and then vehemently claimed as the "natural religion for the black man"—the belief of the Nation of Islam (158; 159),[1] a sect of African American converts. Malcolm X considered that such a community had long been worshiping a God that did not look like "one of their own kind" (166), as Christianity taught them to show devotion to a "blond-haired, blue-eyed Jesus", he complained not without irony (224). The present paper chiefly focuses on the ensuing religious identity through its intercultural implications, i.e. how the cohabitation of faiths affects the identification of converts.

Malcolm X was born to a Christian family. According to his autobiography, his father was a freelance, visiting Baptist preacher (5), and his mother a Seventh-Day Adventist churchgoer (18). He grew up at the outskirt of Lansing, Michigan. But his young adulthood was spent in

---

[1] Henceforth, all parenthetical digits with no date indication refer to the page number in the *Autobiography of Malcolm X*.

Boston, Massachusetts, and then in Harlem, New York City, as is clearly and minutely covered in his book. His involvement at that age in organized crime of gambling, hustling, and drug peddling (87), led to his arrest and subsequent sentence of ten years in prison in 1946. Yet, Malcolm X was released on parole in 1952. Encouraged by his siblings who had been visiting him in jail, he started studying the teachings of the Nation of Islam (158). Once out, he joined the sect and became one of its most fervent and candid mouthpieces, for he believed "very much in the power of words to influence and transform lives" pleads his own daughter, actress Attallah Shabazz, in the Foreword to her father's autobiography (1999, ix; xv). Malcolm X's sermons reflected that he was firmly convinced that the sect had the potential to unify African Americans and give them a sense of self-pride (264).

In this sense, the *Autobiography of Malcolm X* reveals itself as an ineluctable testimonial source of first-hand facts about the cultural changes brought forth by the Nation of Islam not only in the personal life of the author of this self-account but even in the attitudes of the sect's disciples at large. By definition, an autobiography is a narrative about the portrayal or reconstruction of an individual's life experience. It represents a reflection on past events and can therefore serve to gain a better understanding of both the pivotal essence of auto-identification and the interactional context leading to it (Meister 2017). Accordingly, the autobiography under examination becomes a repository of informative evidence reflective of the converts' mindsets foregrounding this religious shift. In all likelihood, this shift seems to yield an identification process of the intercultural type. The outcome thereof takes form as Malcolm X dissertates on how he saw the conversion of his people to the Nation of Islam's faith as a precious opportunity to reshape a new collective identity for their community.

This investigation seeks to de-code the phenomenon of interculturality through the self-descriptive testimony of Malcolm X and his sojourn inside the Nation of Islam. Methodologically, the paper adopts an interpretative narrative inquiry for instructive information about how interculturality operated in the present case. It probes the *Autobiography of Malcolm X*, in light of the theoretical views on interculturation. It first examines the passages in the book that reflect characteristics that are particularly conducive to religious and cultural transformation and evolution. Then it analyzes the aspects of cultural cohabitation and exchange between the two systems of spiritual beliefs in contact, namely Christianity and Islam.

1. Interculturality: Theoretical considerations

In situations of such cultural encounters as those epitomized by the Nation of Islam—à priori based on a mélange of African-American, Christian, and Islamic traditions, the field of inquiry belongs to the disciplinary matter of intercultural psychology. The discipline studies the interface of the social contexts wherein human behaviors develop in such a way that they involve people who seek to adapt progressively to a specific culture and identify accordingly (Guerraoui and Troadec 2000, 8). The main approaches adopted in intercultural psychology are of three types: the cultural perspective, the trans-cultural approach, and a third one devoted to dealing with the transformative consequences in situations involving the encounter of a given culture with another.

The cultural approach tends to confront, compare, connect, or disconnect the data about cultures and attitudes, to understand the related psychological functions and processes (Jahoda 1989, 12). As for the trans-cultural approach, it uses the comparison of cultures as a variable and explores the differences and similarities of the psyche/mind in a sort of universal laboratory, to test the validity of the theories formulated essentially regarding the Western world. From the same perspective, the trans-cultural approach seeks as well to grasp the objective causal laws of psychological reactions and reality (Guerraoui and Troadec 2000, 23). It, thus, focuses more on the interactional side and leaves the actual intercultural aspects frustratingly uninvestigated.

The intercultural aspects are best understood when the investigative focus is put on what significantly emerges from the contact of cultures. To this end, the innovative intercultural approach considers in its integrality each culture among the ones cohabiting in any given social context. It does not label cultures as minor or major. On the contrary, this approach offers to take the specificity and legitimacy of each of the cohabiting cultures for granted, by treating them on equal footing. It tends rather to examine cultural changes from a perspective of negotiation of the cultural adaptation (Denoux 2017; 2016; 1994a; 1994b; Guerraoui 2016; 2009). This approach of intercultural psychology mainly focuses on apprehending the identification of the individuals or groups confronted with a plurality of cultural systems. Its objective is to propose a comprehensive schema as to the relational and institutional processes that stem from the situations of contact between cultures. This approach also applies to all cultural forms, be they of ethnic, national, linguistic, religious, regional, generational, or genre natures, to determine how to deal with the effects engendered by cultural differences (Guerraoui 2016, 213).

Stated differently, this approach is interested in studying the significance of such cultural differences to provide the means likely to explain the adjustment of the people involved in situations of the meeting of cultures. From this perspective, it seems most relevant to be used in exploring the effects of religious conversion. It seems so because this approach is particularly interested in the cultural compromises that develop in the contexts of intercultural relations leading to the emergence of new values, rules, norms, and faiths combined with positive, novel identity strategies. All these strategies would be destined to handle, mitigate, or attenuate the tensions arising from cultural contact. This is what Patrick Denoux, an academic authority in intercultural psychology, calls 'interculturation', to account for the process of partial cultural exchange and transformation that is ignited and carried out during the cultural encounter. In Denoux's view, the outcome of such a process is 'interculturality', a telltale of the birth of a distinct, additional cultural form in its own right.

Being the product of interculturation, interculturality stems from what Denoux calls the "cultural differences 'metabolism'" that consists of the reciprocal integration or "ingestion", in his own wording, of aspects of each other's specific culture for shared identity symbols (2017, 32). Arguably, interculturality manifests itself through the instauration of a common, intermediate cultural space. In such a space of encounter, although each of the cultures in contact tends to preserve itself against any substantial influence of the other or threat perceived in each other's presence, some elements of each other's culture are still appropriated and reinterpreted, at least to meet or deal with potential contextual identification needs (Denoux 2016, 20).

Either concept refers to a new perspective connotative of a process very close to that of assimilation, but one that allows people to situate themselves otherwise, rather deliberately in a specific cultural space of their own making. The process of interculturation has nonetheless virtually nothing to do with that of acculturation, i.e. the mere classical, authoritative assimilation to mainstream culture. Unlike acculturation, interculturation becomes integration into a compound culture, wherein the traits of the initial culture are not altogether abandoned in favour of the culture encountered. On the contrary, the initial cultural traits remain overtly cultivated and sometimes even used in such a way as to reshape parts of the very characteristics of the culture with which they come into contact. In the situation of interculturality, indeed, while the cohabiting cultures safeguard most of their distinctive fundamentals, conjecturally parts of their cultural attributes are transformed, thanks to the mutual processes of cultural exchange, mostly in favour of a common cultural area.[2]

In this sense, interculturation becomes the concept given preference over acculturation to define this form of cultural adaptation, or this type of equitable partial acculturation, so to speak. The process of interculturation has the specificity to involve variations in the cultural aspects, which tend to affect each one of the cultures in contact. Accordingly, interculturation is supposed to be a varying, dual-way process of mutual cultural influence that does not cause any of the cultures coming into contact to disappear in favour of the other. That is why, in similar situations, the concept of acculturation is rejected altogether, at least on three grounds. It is mainly blamed for its ideological considerations, epistemological shortcomings, and the methodological approach in general application to it. Indeed, the study of acculturation often fancifully presupposes the superiority of the mainstream culture. Acculturation is also viewed as a hegemonic process of assimilation in that it imposes the adoption of the majority culture, generally regarded as the one of reference, on the minority groups at the detriment of their own ancestral cultures. That is why, at least for the survey of the situations of cohabiting cultures, the substitute concept of interculturation is much more recommended for its relevance and accuracy (Denoux 2017, 25; Guerraoui 2016, 207-209).

In replacement of acculturation, therefore, interculturation conceives of assimilation, if ever there occurs any of it, rather as an adjustment process that entails superficial changes in the cultural symbols with little or no alteration of the fundamental structures of the ancestral cultural expressions. In situations of cultural heterogeneity, the individuals and groups concerned seek to make room for a shared cultural environment wherein they can evolve in a self-serving identification zone, not without well-observed, constant impacts on the cultural symbols of the common cultural space. Indeed, such an identification zone is dynamically the object of ceaseless revaluations and ensuing modifications. It necessitates everlasting adjustments to meet the need for temporary identities whereby to cope with the difficulties or stress arising from the intercultural encounter. These identification needs are among the fundamental concerns of intercultural studies (Guerraoui 2016, 213).

Therefrom, a cultural mixing emerges that leads to the creation of a third cultural system whose expressions do not define any of the cultures in presence of one another (Guerraoui 2016, 211). The resulting case of

---

[2] For an instructive point of view about interculturality, see the School of Toulouse on the matter, mainly as represented by Denoux and Guerraoui. (Consult the References section.)

interculturality, i.e. the new cultural construct, cannot simply be reducible to the sum of the source cultures in contact, either. Quite the opposite, it becomes a cultural entity of its own, offering separate properties along with reinvented symbols of identification (Damak 2018, 123). The novel symbols yield transformed distinct cultural features that are likely to engender composite cultures, the very ones to be unveiled and surveyed.

2. Application to the autobiographical data: Aspects of interculturality

How does interculturality manifest itself in the *Autobiography of Malcolm X*? And what transpires from the book to indicate a mutating religious cultural identification that would be in constant alteration? The book is essentially a conversion narrative. It tells the story of its author reporting his life's multiple experiences from childhood to international fame. It starts with Malcolm X's childhood describing the atrocious death under questionable circumstances of his father at the hands of white supremacists (10), and his mother's subsequent deteriorating mental health (162). This episode of Malcolm X's life determined his hostile stance about white people and their Christianity he overtly denounced as a religion designed for the distress and "curse of the black man" (Handler 1999, xxvii). It is a stance that Malcolm X confirms throughout his book as he keeps reiterating how he was advised at school to abandon his dream of becoming a lawyer for it was "no realistic goal for a nigger", in the words of his pious white teacher (38; 40; 64; 163; 187; 275; 387).

In the middle, the book mainly addresses Malcolm X's commitment to the Nation of Islam for the tenets of which he spent twelve years, from 1952 to 1963, loyally preaching the sect's belief that Christianity had cut African Americans off from their "true identities, their culture, their history, and even their human dignity" (377). The book also showcases how the author considered that the Christian faith had cut them off from any knowledge of their own past language and religion (165). The book explains as well how he converted to Islam which he recognized as a colorblind religion (166; 345). In addition, the book describes Malcolm X's quick emergence as the sect's obtrusively ubiquitous national spokesman. In this respect, the author further specifies his statement as follows: "I had either originally established or organized" for the Nation of Islam "most of the represented temples" throughout the United States (255; 296). The book then documents his subsequent disillusionment with—and eventual departure from—the sect in March 1964 to build his own religious organization that he named the Muslim Mosque Incorporated

(416).

The last part of the book is devoted to Malcolm X's reconversion to mainstream, Oriental Sunni Islam. How he traveled to the Middle East; how he performed the pilgrimage—hajj in the Islamic holy city of Mecca in April 1964 (331), and how everywhere in the Arab countries he visited, to his delight, he was welcomed and treated "like a brother" by people that, according to him, would have been counted as white in US society (347). And Malcolm X returned to his country from his Eastern and Saudi journey with a reconsidered opinion about human nature (345). Indeed, he began showing more propensities toward reconciliation between his people and white Americans. This newly and overtly expressed stance, should we believe his daughter, represented a "heresy to the Nation of Islam at the time [...] who feared that his way, his leadership, might be a serious threat to their power" (Shabazz 1999, xvi). After Malcolm X had been assassinated in Harlem in February 1965, novelist Alex Haley, one of the closest and most stalwart friends of his and the godfather of his eldest daughter (Shabazz 1999, ix), wrote the epilogue to the *Autobiography of Malcolm X*. Haley's epilogue mainly summarizes the very last days of Malcolm X's life and relates the mobilization triggered by his death and funeral. Subsequently, Haley published the whole book, comprising the version of the autobiography that had been reviewed by Malcolm X himself before his assassination.

3. Evolving transformation

Notably, Malcolm X's performance of the pilgrimage-hajj ritual, according to the mainstream Islamic rite, took place at a relatively late point in his life as a convert. It only happened after he had embraced Oriental Sunni Islam, as is clearly stated in his book (325; 329). This actually represented a radical change that no doubt forever seared his religious-cultural transformation with an indelible mark. Meantime, he would gradually evolve in his new Islamic faith. This progressive path substantially started with the meeting of the person he refers to in his story as "Honorable Elijah Muhammad", who was "a black man, just like us", as Malcolm X had initially been told (162). Muhammad's religious doctrine fundamentally rested both on his own prophet-hood and on the divinity of the initiator of the Nation of Islam, a man who was introduced to Muhammad's followers as the incarnation of God on the earth and who visited his people in America, appearing to them in the guise of the Savior in the person of someone referred to as Master Wallace D. Fard (170-71). Besides, to Muhammad, not only was God a human being, but his true name was also "Allah" (161). Analogously, for the sect, God was also the Messiah—to become subsequently referred to as the "Mahdi", a mysterious personage who had appointed Muhammad "as His Last Messenger to the black people of North America" before he disappeared totally (192; 212; uppercases original). Without pretense, Malcolm X confesses that he initially believed that this messenger "had been divinely sent to our people by Allah Himself" (218), and that he would only later learn that some of the sect's teachings and practices "infuriated the Muslims of the East" (171).

The Islamic-like tenets of the sect's faith also included dietary restrictions, such as no solid food being allowed for breakfast, but only juice and coffee (165). The sect's religious laws included similar and very unusual proscriptions too (198). Malcolm X describes such laws as follows:

> Any fornication was absolutely forbidden in the Nation of Islam. Any eating of the filthy pork, or other injurious or unhealthful foods; any use of tobacco, alcohol, or narcotics. No Muslim who followed Elijah Muhammad could dance, gamble, date, attend movies, or sports, or take long vacations from work. Muslims slept no more than health required. (226)

Seemingly, Malcolm X's specific newly adopted rites varied from the simple appropriation of the mainstream Islamic practices, such as the prohibition of the absorption of pig meat, liquors, and narcotics, to the loose imitation of Oriental Islam in decreeing against sports and other leisure activities that mainstream Islam does not outlaw at all. In reality, the new spiritual obligations followed by Malcolm X mostly ranged from obvious similarities to mere adaptations or pure inventions. At any rate, these new obligations tended for the largest part to undergo incessant mutations, throughout the process of religious transformation, with a continuous revaluation of the related cultural traditions, above all as Malcolm X became closer to Oriental Sunni Islam.

In its entirety, this viewpoint about the evolving, borrowed cultural practices applies as well to the sect's worship rituals. Indeed, the process of religious transformation, concerning many precepts, shifted through several stages. For instance, at first, the ablutions prior to prayers were voluntary, according to the rules of the sect. It was only long afterward, Malcolm X had to admit in his autobiographical account, that the purification of the body, as dictated in Islam for the very same worshiping purposes, became mandatory (197).

Likewise, in the Nation of Islam's places of worship, membership was exclusively reserved for black people. And initially, even in Malcolm X's religious organization, the one he created after he had left the sect, all the same, no white people were admitted there, except sometimes for journalists and reporters (323). But the epilogue of this testimony informs the reader that Malcolm X finally changed his mind concerning this form of reversed segregation, so to speak. He at the same time apologetically abandoned his virulent diatribes against his fellow white compatriots and eventually invited them for a rapprochement and rehabilitative dialogue (402).

In close regard, Malcolm X relinquished his Christian patronymic in stages as well. He first followed the sect's instructions to abandon the family name of "Little" which he considered having been imposed on his paternal forebears. He instead adopted the sect's "X", a symbol of the lost original ancestral name, he regretfully points out, that the African American could never retrieve (203). Afterward, he Arabicized his name altogether into Malik—instead, but still reminiscent, of Malcolm—El-Shabazz. And finally, he became identified as El-Hajj Malik El-Shabazz (349), with the honorific title indicative of someone who had performed the Islamic, Koranic pilgrimage. It was so affixed to his new name, as though to signify that he at long last gained the recognition of Eastern Muslims.

4. Impact of cohabitation: Unilateral influence

In the same vein, Malcolm X spent the largest part of his life as a convert saying his Islamic prayers in English. "In Elijah Muhammad's Nation of Islam, we hadn't prayed in Arabic", he remarks disapprovingly (335). Besides, in his autobiographical narrative, the reader discovers that just rudiments of the Arabic language are used, if any, generally to serve the Nation of Islam's specific proselytism. Therein, the use of Arabic is very much restricted either to such words as "Allah", to refer to God, or in the roughly transcribed greeting expression of "*As-Salaam Alaikum*"—Peace Be unto you, or yet the praising call of "*Allahu-Akbar*"—Allah is the Greatest (197-8). Malcolm X, for one, only began to learn how to pray in Arabic in 1964 (349). "Today," he confirms in his book, "I say with my family in the Arabic tongue the prayer which I first learned in English" (198).

The same can be said in terms of religious-cultural influence on the design and ornamentation inside the sect's payer facilities (199). The interior was organized church-like, in halls, with rows of pews or folding chairs, altar, etc. (217). Malcolm X, unaccustomed to the orthodox Islamic prayer posture, would eventually end up learning the conventional prayer ritual, i.e. on rags, laid flat on the floor in rudimentary decorated places (349). This was not achieved without physical difficulties, however, for "Western ankles won't do what Muslim ankles have done for a lifetime", he cunningly explains in his *Autobiography*. (333).

Similarly, in his capacity as a leader in the sect of the Nation of Islam, Malcolm X used to conduct funeral ceremonies. Although he cut with the Christian obligations of flowers, singing, and organ playing, traditionally offered in respectful farewell to the deceased, he still had to follow the sect's instructions of mixing Islamic and biblical obituary recitals. This is best illustrated in his own reminder as follows:

> I would start by reading over the casket of the departed brother or sister a prayer to Allah. [...] Then I usually read from Job; two passages, in the seventh and fourteenth chapters, where Job speaks of no life after death. Then another passage where David, when his son died, spoke also of no life after death. [...] But I was to learn later that ... the funeral service was in drastic contradiction to what Islam taught in the East. (228)

In Malcolm X's opinion, references to the New Testament were not occasional or episodic in the prayer services led by the preachers of the Nation of Islam, (168). Quite the opposite, they often abided by the sect's teachings about "the interrelated meanings and uses of the Bible and the Quran" (215). This mixture of both religious traditions would follow Malcolm X to his funeral service, although it proceeded according to an entirely dissimilar pattern. His funeral actually involved two services that took place in a church, nonetheless, in the same Faith Temple Church of God in Christ. The first one was celebrated there in accordance with the Christian rites by Bishop Alvin A. Childs, with a protracted ceremonial and a floral wreath arrangement (Haley 1999, 450; 461). The second service observed the orthodox Islamic custom, with a short prayer recited in that very church by Sheik Ahmed Hassoun, a Sudanese spiritual and pedagogical advisor at the Muslim Mosque Incorporated, Malcolm X's religious organization. Sheik Hassoun preliminarily had prepared the body for burial by removing the Western suit and tie in which the deceased's remains had been on display in the open coffin previously, and then by washing and draping the corpse in the conventional Islamic white linen shroud (Haley 1999, 459).

Despite efforts at adjustment, therefore, several original Christian practices were adamantly maintained even after conversion. The Nation of Islam called its preachers "Ministers"; and, it used to name its prayer facilities "temples", at least until 1961, when by order of Elijah Muhammad the sect began adopting the more canonical designation of "mosques"

(268). However, the appellation Minister—never Imam—remained (269), as did many other Christian rituals and traditions. Indeed, prayer meetings in congregation were held on Sundays, not on Fridays (198; 223), as invariably in Muslim societies. The sect also maintained the passing of the plates or buckets at the ends of the services for collecting donations (217; 261), a habit seldom to be seen in Oriental mosques, as the organizational and administrative expenses thereof are generally assumed by political or local authorities.

Notwithstanding all this, in the stories largely confided to his autobiography, curiously, Malcolm X makes no mention whatsoever of the rite of fasting in any of the religious cultures involved. Yet, total or partial imitations of the attitudes and apparel of Oriental Muslims do abound. They sometimes border on superficial symbolic representations of Islamic cultural identity. The reader learns, for instance, that the sect's spiritual teacher, always in public wore a fez with a golden embroidery featuring the crescent and star, an epitome of Islamic culture (200); or that Malcolm X had grown a goatee, as a beard destined to announce his conversion to Islam (192); or yet that he believed in destiny and Allah's protection and that "everything is *written*" (152; emphasis added), as the common belief goes in traditional Middle-Eastern communities.

5. Findings and interpretation

The point underscoring the present inquiry is to know whether Malcolm X's spiritual stance could reflect an identification of the intercultural type, i.e. precisely one likely to yield interculturality as a new cultural construct. It was evidently the case, as the religion of the Nation of Islam that he followed, during the largest part of his life as a convert, proposed a revisited version of the Islamic faith that incorporated tenets and rituals from two religions. Admittedly, this revisited version borrowed basically from Islam; but it relied to a non-negligible extent on Christianity too. By extension, Malcolm X was offered both corresponding religious cultures whence he could draw the composite substance of his new spiritual identification.

Arguably, it was through religious appropriation and cultural adaptation that the Nation of Islam managed to transform the spiritual identity symbols. In so doing, the sect created a situation propitious for the initiation of a process of interculturation. This process involved the deliberate juxtaposition of two faiths in the same space of interaction. In the case under examination, interculturality, the product of such a cohabitation, emerges through the antithetical, sometimes evolving coexistence of discernable Islamic characteristics with manifest Western Christian aspects and settings. No doubt, in that space, there cohabited the church, the temple, and the mosque; all three of which shared customs and rituals in an incessant development of piecemeal cultural mutation. In exchange for the appropriation of Islamic rituals, the undeniable influence of Christianity was preserved. It fundamentally led to the metamorphosis of the host Islamic religion by mere incorporation—not to say ingestion— of Christian traditions, in a move of cultural metabolism, to invoke but Denoux's metaphorical representation of interculturality.

In the present case, as it stems from Malcolm X's autobiographical testimony, interculturality reveals itself, in part, through the display of distinctive Islamic practices in a prevailing Christian environment. On the other hand, interculturality manifests itself through the obvious influence that such an environment can have on the rituals of the newly adopted faith. In this case, indeed, the Christian traditions interculturally permeated the sect's Islamic rites wherein not only the tongues mingled but also the scriptures, the designations, and the decorative arrangements of worshiping venues.

Besides, the converts' choice did reflect an expression of interculturality because it adequately emanated from two faiths sharing the same space of interaction. Yet, although it was definitely the direct outcome of a process of partial transformation and adaptation of religious practices, interculturality allowed these people—here disciples—to maintain a sense of simultaneous connectedness to both their hereditary religious culture and the faith they converted to, apparently in pursuit of a comfortable form of worship that encompassed either one of them.

On top of that, the interculturality resulting from this interfaith contact only relied on superficial and formal aspects. Indeed, in this religious-cultural cohabitation, the authentic fundamental structures of both religions remained unchanged, in confirmation of the theoretical views about the tendency of the residual differences to resist any transformation whatsoever.

However, even though in this case interculturality undeniably constituted a real zone of reciprocal overlapping symbols of identification from the two cohabiting religions, it did not involve a dual-way process of interculturation, as is frequently suggested by the theoretical views about it. In other words, no actual, mutual cultural exchange took place in this case. It was rather a unilateral influence. Obviously, in this respect, it was the Christian traditions that alone overlapped over the Islamic practices and not the other way around.

Even so, religious conversion did generate a third space of a genuine intercultural mix with two cultural systems in contact. This created a hybrid religious culture that was neither totally ancestral nor completely alien, and neither wholly Islamic nor entirely Christian. In the final analysis, such a third space did nonetheless yield a cultural entity of its own that still lent support to the intercultural nature of the identification symbols sought after by the disciples of the sect.

Conclusion

Admittedly, conversion to a religion—altogether different from the prevalent one—offers a typical illustration of interculturality. It triggers a process of interculturation that entails constant ritual changes that combine with the remnants of the relinquished faith to give birth to a new one. This results in the conspicuous initiation of a third spiritual intercultural zone of identification. The *Autobiography of Malcolm X* harbors enough information indicating that the religious life experienced by this book's author, a convert himself, unquestionably represented—and still represents— a case in point.

Arguably, through the observed case, it turns out that interculturality is a dynamic phenomenon par excellence. When it comes to religious conversion, not only does interculturality involve the free imitation of spiritual injunctions and reutilization of established cultural traditions, but it also remains subject to incessant revaluation and mutation in a perpetual process of revision of rituals and practices.

What remains to be determined is the rationale for this deliberate change of faith. What lurked actually behind the creation of such a third religious zone of the intercultural type, while the other distinctive original cultural traits were rather preserved and continued to be claimed as the foundation of one's social and national identities? A prospective answer would have recourse to the social psychological theories tending to identity behaviors. The rationale might well be a strategy of making public one's rejection of the imposed religious culture and thereby suggesting one's own terms of social inclusion and national integration. Or it might well be an ethnic reaction, rather; one that would utilize the religious identity dimension as a protective shield against the adversity perceived in the social context of interaction in an attempt to eschew discrimination. This should invite a rereading of Malcolm X's autobiographical story, preferably from an interactional, cultural anthropological perspective.

References

Damak, Sadok. 2018. "Interculturation and Ethnicity: 'Spanglish' as the Emergence of a Third Identity." In The Poetics and Politics of Identity, edited by Chantal Zabus, Ezzeddine Saidi, and Jawhar A. Dhouib, 111-25. Gabes, Tunisia: TAELS Publications.

Denoux, Patrick. 2017. "En finir avec l'interculturel polymorphe: L'interculturation, un concept générique." In Cognition sociale, formes d'expression et interculturalité, edited by Ghazi Chakroun, 25-37. Paris: L'Harmattan.

—. 2016. "Préface." In L'interculturel aujourd'hui: Perspectives et enjeux, edited by Élisabeth Regnault and Élaine Costa-Fernandez, 19-26. Paris: L'Harmattan.

—. 1994a. "L'identité interculturelle." Bulletin de Psychologie 419 (xlviii-6-9): 264-70.

—. 1994b. "Pour une nouvelle définition de l'interculturation." In Perspectives de l'interculturel, edited by Jeannine Blomart and Bernd Krewer, 67-81. Paris: L'Harmattan.

Guerraoui, Zohra. 2016. "L'interculturation: Pour une autre approches des contacts de culture." In L'interculturel aujourd'hui: Perspectives et enjeux, edited by Élisabeth Regnault and Élaine Costa-Fernandez, 207-16. Paris: L'Harmattan.

—. 2009. "De l'acculturation à l'interculturation: Réflexions épistémologiques." L'Autre, Clinique, Cultures et Sociétés, 10 N°2: 195-200.

Guerraoui, Zohra, and Bertrand Troadec. 2000. Psychologie interculturelle. Paris: Armand Colin.

Haley, Alex. 1999. "Epilogue." In The Autobiography of Malcolm X: As Told to Alex Haley, edited by Malcolm X, 390-463. New York: Ballantine Books.

Handler, Michael. S. 1999. "Introduction." In The Autobiography of Malcolm X: As Told to Alex Haley, edited by Malcolm X, xxv-xxx. New York: Ballantine Books.

Jahoda, Gustav. 1989. Psychologie et anthropologie. Paris: Armand Colin.

Meister, Daniel R. 2017. "The Biographical Turn and The Case for Historical Biography." History Compass 16, No. 2 (Dec.): 1-10. https://doi.org/10.1111/hic3.12436

Shabazz, Attallah. 1999. "Foreword." In The Autobiography of Malcolm X: As Told to Alex Haley, edited by Malcolm, X, ix-xxiv. New York: Ballantine Books.

X, Malcolm. 1999. The Autobiography of Malcolm X: As Told to Alex Haley. New York: Ballantine Books.

CHAPTER 7

DAVID CAMERON'S ACCOUNT OF THE BREXIT REFERENDUM: WHAT DOES IT BRING FORTH?

FATHI BOURMECHE

Introduction

The aim of this chapter is to throw more light on the Brexit referendum held on 23 June 2016, resulting in Britain's exit from the European Union (henceforth, EU), which put an end to more than forty years of partnership between Europe and Britain. The intention is to gain a better understanding of the Brexit campaign through David Cameron's lenses, having then been Prime Minister and one of the leading figures in the Remain camp. Attention is paid to Cameron's own narrative, as revealed in his autobiography entitled *For the Record*, the case of chapter 46, "Referendum". The assumption is that the chapter provides a first-hand account of the different events and circumstances under Cameron's premiership during the referendum.

A qualitative analysis is conducted following Coffey's (2014) approach in her study "Analysing Documents," appearing in Uwe Flick's *The Sage Handbook of Qualitative Data Analysis*. In Coffey's (2014) view, autobiographies, considered among the documents for social research purposes, are significant in terms of their revelations about different issues, including settings and lives. The analysis is focused on Cameron's version of the whole campaign, subsequently marking his loss of the gamble, thus offering the Leave camp the opportunity to occupy the British political scene for a while.

Particular attention is paid to the main themes and arguments presented in Cameron's narrative in the hope of gaining a better insight into the twists and turns of the Brexit campaign, starting with an obvious lead for the Remain camp, slightly shrinking before the exit polls. Nevertheless, the Leave camp won with a slight majority, putting the stakes high on the future of both the EU and Britain. The current study seeks to argue that Cameron's own version of the Brexit campaign seems to be a confession by the former prime minister about what went wrong during the campaign, leading to a victory of the Leave camp, including Boris Johnson, a popular politician among the Conservatives and one of the potential successors to Cameron. In this sense, Cameron's first-hand account of the whole event, including the obstacles that his team encountered during the referendum campaign, provides a detailed narrative of Brexit, offering new perspectives on a significant episode in the history of the country. Coffey (2014) contends that such a type of document has documentary realities, including intimate and personal relationships as well as public ones. In view of this, Cameron's account could provide a better insight into Brexit, unveiling some of the realities about such a significant event.

Indeed, findings of the study showed that Cameron's version of the Brexit referendum was centred around four major issues, all of which offered a better insight into the whole event through a detailed record of the different debates and controversies over the campaign. The first issue is Cameron's struggle to keep his close friends among his inner team, namely Michael Gove and Johnson, two Eurosceptic Conservatives. The second issue is related to Gove and Johnson's desertion and more divisions within the Conservative Party, given that a significant number of Conservatives resigned during the campaign. The third issue is associated with Brexit as a common ground campaign with a cross-party support, missing to address immigration. In other words, Cameron's Remain camp was joined by politicians from different political parties and affiliations, including Jeremy Corbyn, Labour leader, gaining cross-party support, though, unlike the Leave camp, missed to tackle immigration, particularly from the EU. The fourth issue is linked to Cameron's relationship with the media, the campaign's final day and his revelations about the Remain loss, highlighting the Prime Minister's reactions and feelings while waiting for the Brexit results, in addition to some moving stories from his family.

1. Cameron's struggle to keep his close friends among his inner team

Cameron revealed the different controversies and tensions between his close friends during the campaign, emphasising his concern about losing their support in the course of Brexit. His major concern from the beginning was that his inner team, including Gove and Johnson, would not stand by his side throughout the campaign. Gove, known as a journalist for the *Times* and a prominent politician holding different positions, was part of Cameron's Cabinet, being Lord Chancellor and Secretary for Justice from May 2015 to July 2016. Similarly, Johnson, a former journalist and Mayor of London, before leaving his post and becoming spokesman for the Leave camp, was one of Cameron's close friends.

Cameron's concern about losing his friends' support was clearly stated when he met families and friends at Chequers on New Year's Eve, with Gove and Sara Vine among his guests. Vine, a columnist for the *Daily Mail*, was Gove's wife then, (though they would split in 2021 after 20 years of marriage and two children). Cameron addressed Vine to show his worries about division among the Conservatives, with potential Leave supporters and Remain ones. By addressing Vine, Cameron confessed that he was interested in Gove's stance, being aware of the latter's strong Euroscepticism. He recalled that Gove had argued that Britons should not be worried about their life outside the EU. Cameron's worries were legitimate, as Gove's argument was just the opposite of Cameron's throughout the Brexit campaign, insisting that Britain would be stronger in Europe. But Vine assured him that Gove would be supportive all through, in which he believed then. Therefore, he decided to turn his attention to Johnson while asking George Osborne, then Chancellor of the Exchequer, to take care of Gove, given his suspicion over the two men's support.

Cameron believed that Gove and Johnson's joining the Leave camp would be very harmful to his campaign, arguing that "these two front-liners would legitimise the cause and help detoxify the Brexit brand" (Cameron 2019, chap. 46). Indeed, Cameron seemed aware of the popularity of these two figures among the Conservatives in the case of Gove, and among the British public in the case of Johnson, seen as the most popular politician in Britain. Although the polls were then showing support for Cameron, the Prime Minister believed that when these two influential figures left his camp, both their popularity and intellectual heft would significantly change the polls in favour of the Leave side. Cameron emphasised that some polls predicted that with Johnson on his side, the Remain camp would have an 8 per cent lead. But if Johnson joined the Leave camp, such a lead would drop to 1 per cent. Other polls went further by predicting that the Remain lead would be halved if Johnson joined the Leave camp, implying the weight of such a figure in relation to Brexit results.

Following Osborne's talk with Gove, Cameron pointed out that his worries were more than real. Therefore, he decided that he would join Osborne in the next conversation with Gove. When they met on the yellow sofas of the Downing Street flat, Cameron reminded Gove of their achievements both in opposition and in power, in addition to the possible radical changes after securing a majority government in 2015. Cameron emphasised the fact that Gove came back to power with his favourite position, namely Secretary of Justice, allowing him to reform prisons in the country. Cameron's intention was obviously to avoid putting his campaign in jeopardy by trying to prevent Gove from joining the Leave camp. In the words of Osborne, Britain's exit from the EU would be fatal not only to the country but also to their team, as part of the Remain camp, by putting an end to their political careers, including the Prime Minister's.

In Cameron's view, Gove seemed bewildered because he did not yet make up his mind about joining the Leave camp. But he promised to deliver no more than one speech in support of Brexit, denying any other contribution to the campaign. Nevertheless, Cameron could not believe that Gove, one of his inner team and a close confidant to whom he would turn for advice, would not remain on his side throughout the campaign. Although Cameron was aware of Gove's strong Euroscepticism, he did not expect him to sacrifice his loyalty to the team with which he had been working. Yet, Cameron admitted that he trusted Gove's words by promising not to play a significant role when joining the Leave camp.

The other close friend, Johnson, was badly needed in the Prime Minister's team, being a former journalist, whose talent was much respected. Cameron believed in him for his talents would allow him to benefit the government by running a big department. Cameron recalled that he knew about Johnson's Euroscepticism as well, dating back to his days as a reporter in Brussels for the *Telegraph* when he had strongly supported the idea of a referendum, particularly in relation to the Lisbon Treaty.[1] Cameron pointed out that he had numerous conversations with Johnson on Europe, but he never heard him argue for leaving the EU. Yet, Cameron decided to meet him at the American ambassador's court where they could play and talk privately. After the game was over, Cameron started talking about how close they were in terms of ideology, an idea emphasised by Johnson at their party conference held in October 2016. Moreover, Cameron claimed that Johnson, Osborne and himself were virtually interchangeable, as revealed in each one's speech delivered at the conference, though nobody had had any idea about the content of the other's speech. The implication is that Johnson was, similar to Gove, part

---

[1] The Treaty started as a constitutional project in 2001 and was followed up in 2002 and 2003 by the European Convention which drafted the Treaty establishing a Constitution for Europe (https://www.europarl.europa.eu/factsheets/en/sheet/5/the-treaty-of-lisbon).

of his inner team and therefore Cameron strongly believed that he was indispensable for the Remain camp.

Cameron admitted that, although Johnson was dissatisfied with the outcome of the EU renegotiations of Britain's status within the EU preceding the referendum,[2] he did not expect him to vote leave. Cameron also confessed that, in the hope of keeping Johnson on his side throughout the campaign, he promised to offer him one of the top five ministries with a Remain win. As Cameron had no intention to remove Osborne as Chancellor of the Exchequer, he hinted at the Defence Department for Johnson, believing that it would prevent his withdrawal from his inner team. He went even further by tempting Johnson that he could potentially be the next prime minister should a contest take place between him and Osborne, given that Cameron had no intention to have another premiership. Although he did not hide his strong support for Osborne, Cameron showed Johnson that he would fit the premiership.[3]

Cameron highlighted the fact that Johnson's attitudes towards sovereignty of UK laws over the EU ones were minor issues compared to his inner thoughts about the image that he would gain as a prominent figure in the Leave camp. This is clearly articulated in the following statement:

> I could almost see his thought process take shape. Whichever senior Tory politician took the lead on the Brexit side – so loaded with images of patriotism, independence and romance – would become the darling of the party. He didn't want to risk allowing someone else with a high profile – Michael Gove in particular – to win that crown (Cameron 2019, chap. 46).

The above statement reveals Cameron's capacity to read Johnson's psyche and his love to leadership and prestige. Indeed, Johnson's intentions proved to be right after joining the Leave camp, showing a strong sense of patriotism and nationalism. Johnson was behaving as a nationalist leader throughout the campaign and in its aftermath, focusing on British sovereignty against Brussels' domination.

---

[2] Cameron believed that the agreement reached at the European Council meeting (18 and 19 February 2016) on Britain's relationship with the EU was satisfactory in relation to his letter sent in November 2015 to ask for a "special status" for his country. But many politicians, including people among his cabinet, did not like the new terms because such an agreement did not settle most of the controversial issues, including EU migration.

[3] Ironically, neither Osborne nor Johnson would be Cameron's successor, it was rather Theresa May, the second female prime minister in the country after Margaret Thatcher, following Cameron's resignation in the aftermath of Brexit.

However, Cameron understood that Johnson was sure that Brexiteers would lose. Therefore, choosing to support the Leave camp would have little risk of damaging the government that he would like to lead in the near future. Cameron recalled that he repeatedly warned Johnson against choosing the wrong path, namely siding with the Leave camp, being aware that Johnson was "torn between his head telling him that leaving would be a mistake, and his heart telling him to lead the romantic case for greater independence" (Cameron 2019, chap. 46). Cameron, recognizant of Johnson's willingness to seize the Brexit opportunity without losing his political career, failed to persuade him to be on his side all through.

Cameron's two close friends, namely Gove and Johnson, would write him an open letter following the release (on 26 May 2016) of the Office for National Statistics (ONS) figures, showing an all-time high record of net migration, reaching 333,000 in 2015. Both Gove and Johnson were critical of Cameron's pledge to reduce net migration to the tens of thousands. Johnson went further in an interview by considering such a pledge as a scandal made by politicians, which shocked Cameron. According to the Prime Minster, it was a pledge which had been worked out as part of a manifesto all of who had been elected on, including his two close friends. In this sense, both Gove and Johnson, part of Cameron's inner team, had abandoned the rules of engagement and started an open warfare.

2. Gove and Johnson's desertion and more divisions among the Conservatives

Apart from his two close friends, Cameron was also concerned about more desertions among his cabinet members, which would lead to a significant split among the Conservatives. Cameron pointed out that he, along with Osborne, repeatedly met members of the Cabinet, having been determined to have a chance with everyone to make sure who would be supportive throughout the campaign. Although he knew that some, including Chris Grayling, Theresa Villiers, Iain Duncan Smith and John Whittingdale, would certainly join the Leave camp, he hoped that, by meeting all of them, he would persuade some to be on his side all through the referendum. Cameron recalled that Osborne managed to gain the support of Sajid Javid whose pro-Brexit stance was unexpected to the Prime Minister. Javid was then a prominent politician from a British Pakistani family, the first non-white Briton holding various Cabinet positions under a Conservative government. During the Brexit campaign, he served as

Secretary of State for Business, Innovation and Skills (from May 2015 until July 2016).

Cameron, on his part, was not able to persuade Priti Patel who was then Minister of State for Employment, having been a strong advocate of leaving the EU. Cameron contended that he was even shocked by Patel after her article for the *Telegraph* on 28 May 2016, criticising "wealthy leaders of Remain, who could never know the downsides of immigration" (Cameron 2019, chap. 46). In Cameron's view, such an argument was merely a criticism of the Conservative manifesto on which she had herself been elected, becoming member of his Cabinet. Although Patel subsequently carried on her critical views over the government's failure to handle immigration, Cameron admitted that he was not able to fire her. Had he done so, Patel would become a Brexit martyr, fuelling the ongoing psychodrama among the Conservatives while the Prime Minister was trying to stop it then. More about the immigration issue is further developed in the following section.

However, Cameron managed to persuade Liz Truss, then Secretary of State for Environment, Food and Rural Affairs and Jeremy Wright, then Attorney General and Secretary of State for Digital, Culture, Media and Sport, both of who had been hesitant. Cameron confessed that the "latent Leaver gene in the Tory Party was more dominant than" (Cameron 2019, chap. 46) he had personally imagined. The Prime Minister recalled that his conservation with Duncan Smith was quite interesting, as the latter started by expressing his satisfaction with his job in government, focusing on domestic affairs and tackling poverty. But he then turned his attention to Europe on the first occasion, ushering in more divisions among the Conservatives.

Cameron became fully aware that the split in his party, initially expected to be 70-30, would grow to almost 50-50, although he was unable to make any predictions about who would be quickest to start such a split. The Prime Minster pointed out that while he was still in Brussels to seal the deal on which he had agreed with his European counterparts, Gove was the first one to condemn such a deal. At his special cabinet meeting after his Brussels visit, Cameron discovered that his ten-year endeavour to keep his party united was in tatters, with his colleagues holding conflicting views on Europe. At the meeting, which was meant to discuss a few issues related to their stance on the EU, including fixing a date for the referendum, Cameron listened to both Leavers and Remainers, learning about their arguments for their choice, though Leavers agreed on Cameron's deal in Brussels. Cameron reminded all his team that they needed to fulfil their duties as elected members by the British voters irrespective of their stance.

Immediately after the meeting, Cameron revealed that the split was enormous, as reported by Sky News. Gove was followed by Duncan Smith, Grayling, Patel, Villiers and Whittingdale, all of who lined up at Vote Leave headquarters, appearing for Cameron as a parallel cabinet. Such a cabinet was led by Gove who would be crowned as 'co-convenor' with Gisela Stuart, Labour MP. Cameron recalled that Gove would later be omnipresent for any Leave camp event, occasionally arguing that Britain's membership to the EU was dangerous. The implication is that Gove proved to be a liar, i.e. not keeping his word, given that he had already promised Cameron that he would not play a major role when joining the Leave camp, as aforementioned. In this view, Cameron seemed to have been betrayed by his closest friend during the campaign.

At this stage, Johnson did not yet leave Cameron's team, though admitted to the British press that he was swerving like a broken shopping trolley because he did not make up his mind yet about which side to support. Johnson was updating Cameron about his state of mind, constantly vacillating. Such a vacillation was seen in his writing two different opinions, one for out and one for in Europe. He subsequently left Cameron's team, informing him that Brexit "would be crushed 'like the toad beneath the harrow'," adding "that he couldn't look himself in the mirror if he campaigned to remain" (Cameron 2019, chap. 46). Johnson's desertion would be a serious blow for Cameron who confessed that Johnson's favourability rate as a leading politician was higher than his, which would potentially have a significant impact on attracting soft voters. Cameron considered both Gove and Johnson's departure from his inner team as a defection of two military leaders at the very beginning of the battle.

Cameron argued that Gove would later have "his hands dirty," with harsh criticism over the renegotiation deal signed with the EU, claiming that such a deal could be overridden by the European Court of Justice. Gove's claim, a shock to the Prime Minister, would be debunked by Cameron's team of lawyers as well as the Attorney General, given that a deal signed by the 28-member states would have the same legal force as any other treaty. Nevertheless, Cameron admitted that the Remain camp was losing credibility, compared to the Leave camp, particularly due to Gove's attitudes towards experts among Remainers. In Cameron's view, Gove, "one of the most learned, empirical people [he] knew, had suddenly become an ambassador for the post-truth age" (Cameron 2019, chap. 46). Obviously, Cameron's statement was highly critical of not only his close friends but also of the Leave camp, particularly for their dependence on figures such as saving billions of pounds of their contribution to the EU and spending them on the NHS (National Health Service) instead. Their pledge was to save £350 million on a weekly basis for the NHS by leaving the EU, proved later unrealistic and farther from the truth.

To Cameron's shock, Gove would later appear among Leavers who launched a poster warning that Turkey whose population counted 76 million would join the EU. Cameron did not expect Gove, "the liberal-minded, carefully considered Conservative intellectual [to become] a foam-flecked Faragist"[4] (Cameron 2019, chap. 46) threatening British voters over the influx of Turkish people. What was even worse for Cameron was the fact that Johnson, who had traditionally been proud of his Turkish heritage and a strong advocate of Turkey's EU membership, turned into a supporter of the false claims about the country's accession. Such attitudes for Cameron could heighten concern about Islam, speculating that the Leave camp might use the slogan "If you want a Muslim for a neighbour, vote Remain," echoing the slogan raised in Smethwick in the 1964 by-election.[5]

In addition to Gove's withdrawal, Cameron pointed out that learning about Duncan Smith's resignation, after his return from a European Council meeting, was harmful to the left-right balance of the government. Cameron's several calls with him, in the hope of preventing such a resignation, were in vain. Although, Cameron had the impression that Duncan Smith softened while he was still on the phone trying to convince him to stay, Sky News broadcast the resignation. Significantly, Cameron knew about the second resignation from the media. (More about Cameron's relationship with the media is elaborated later.) Apart from Gove and Johnson, two of his closest Conservatives, Cameron was shocked by the attitudes of four veterans among his party, Norman Lamont, Nigel Lawson, Michael Howard, in addition to Duncan Smith, all of who accused Remainers in a letter published in the *Daily Telegraph* of frightening British voters. Such defections seemed to have had a major impact on the integrity of the Conservative Party during the Brexit campaign, marking a significant friction within that Party.

---

[4] This refers to Nigel Farage, then leader of UKIP (United Kingdom Independence Party), a nationalist, far-right political formation. Not unexpectedly, Farage was one of the main figures in the Leave camp.

[5] Conservative Peter Griffiths secured the constituency, defeating Labour in spite of his supporters' slogan "'If you want a nigger neighbour, vote Labour'" (Paul 1997, 177).

3. Brexit: A common ground campaign with a cross-party support missing to address immigration

In Cameron's view, the campaign represented an occasion where the two major parties, Labour and the Conservatives, as well as the other parties, would fight on a common ground. From the start, Cameron believed that they would be winners-in-waiting of their *Stronger In* campaign. It was, therefore, decided to give the leadership of the campaign to two Labour MPs: Peter Mandelson and Will Straw (son of Jack Straw, former Labour Home Secretary under Prime Minister Gordon Brown) and the steering to the Conservatives. Cameron recalled that their Sunday evening meetings at Downing Street had been reinstated not only for his cabinet but also for all the cross-party members of the Remain camp. For the Prime Minister, it seemed that they were doing better than Brexiteers, given that they managed to gain a cross-party consensus on their campaign, compared to their opponents; the latter were unable to make up their mind about one single name, swaying from terms like *Vote Leave*, *Leave* and *Grassroots Out*, in addition to their controversy over leadership.

Cameron was confident that by the end of April, i.e. with two months left to the referendum, Remainers gained a near-unanimous cross-party support, along with a large number of MPs. Such a support, in Cameron's view, was reinforced by various government resources and unprecedented experts, emphasising their six-year experience in power, a period known for two significant victories. The first one was a victory in the 2014 Scottish referendum, held to decide for the future of Scotland within the UK. The Scottish referendum, initiated by Nicola Sturgeon, then leader of the Scottish National Party (SNP), resulted in a majority of Scottish people voting to remain within the UK, thus avoiding a significant split in the kingdom. The second one was a strong majority for the Conservatives in the House of Commons in the 2015 general election after their coalition government with Liberal Democrats (then led by Nik Clegg) following a weak majority in the 2010 British general election. With such an experience, Cameron believed, Remainers would appeal to a large number of voters.

However, Cameron pointed out that despite the cross-party clout reliance on Labour, the Opposition were inefficient in that they did not appear very active throughout the campaign. Cameron recalled that although Corbyn contributed to the campaign through a few speeches about Remain, the latter did not attend all the significant events, occasionally leaving for a holiday instead. In other words, Cameron was dissatisfied with Labour's efforts during the campaign despite the fact that his team had already allotted whole days for Labour politicians. Such an inefficiency made voters think of Cameron as the major advocate of Remain rather than Corbyn. Cameron claimed that voters would even think of Barak Obama, then US President, and Mark Carney, then Bank of England Governor, as Remainers before any thoughts about Corbyn.

Cameron had even thought of the idea that Corbyn wanted Remainers to lose, given his anti-capitalist views, having seen the EU as a trading organisation, in addition to his voting leave back in the 1975 referendum. In Cameron's view, Corbyn might have thought that Brexit would damage the Conservatives in the way the 2008 financial crisis had damaged Labour. The Prime Minister reiterated Corbyn's absence from some great moments during the campaign. For example, in one of the speeches at the Oval cricket ground, Cameron was next to a blue Mini, Tim Farron, Leader of the Liberal Democrats was next to a yellow one, and Natalie Bennett, Leader of the Greens was next to a green Brompton bike, but Corbyn was missing. Cameron claimed that such a speech was meant to show a visual representation of unity among British political parties which had joined the Remain camp. However, Corbyn's absence was a major hindrance to such an impact.

Yet, there were some instances of unity among Remainers, particularly Labour and the Conservatives, with the appearance of John Major, former Conservative Prime Minister (1990-1997) and Tony Blair, former Labour Prime Minister (1997-2007) in Northern Ireland. Such an appearance was meant to emphasise the risks of leaving the EU, evoking the impact on the peace process in the region as well as on the Irish border. One of the major arguments used against Brexit was the imposition of hard borders between Northern Ireland and the Republic of Ireland, which would inflame tensions between the two parts and thus ending peace. However, Cameron felt that they were unable to deliver in relation to immigration, particularly from the EU, one of the most controversial issues focused upon by Brexiteers.

Cameron expressed his dissatisfaction with the way the media covered EU migration, particularly from the perspectives of Brexiteers. For example, Gove argued (on 20 May 2016) that EU migration would result in the influx of five million people by 2030, pointing to the EU's intention of adding Albania, Macedonia, Montenegro, Serbia and Turkey. Cameron confessed that, although Brexiteers were not telling the truth on Turkey, they were right on raising the issue of immigration. The Prime Minister was aware of soaring immigration, ridiculing his repeated pledge to reduce net migration to the tens of thousands. Such a pledge was debunked by the ONS figures on net migration mentioned above.

Cameron claimed that one obvious solution to curb net migration would be to put an end to free mobility by leaving the EU. Yet, he believed that the issue was more complex than one could imagine in the sense that half of the migrants were from outside the EU, emphasising the benefit of migration to the UK economy, attracting different workers to its growing labour market. However, Cameron's perspective on EU migration was challenged by ordinary people's perspectives following a BBC Yorkshire studio he was watching once. In a five-minute package about the arrival of Slovakians to Rotherham, presented in the programme, inhabitants there expressed their willingness to leave the area. Their move was explained by the fact that the new arrivals were usurping their parks and public areas, turning the whole region to a mess. Moreover, locals complained that they had never voted to accept such an influx. By hearing such arguments from lay men, Cameron discovered how simple the Brexiteers' stance about immigration was, compared to theirs about the economy. It was then that he became aware of his potential failure on this matter, particularly EU migration.

Cameron's team could not reach a consensus on the way to address such an issue. Some suggested that they should make a full case on immigration; others suggested a new pledge to curb the number of new arrivals. As for Labour politicians within the team, the idea was to create a fund for regions affected by mass migration. Some others suggested to renegotiate the matter with Angela Merkel, then German Chancellor, threatening her to leave the EU if they did not relax immigration to Britain. In other words, they would like to reduce free mobility and thus curb EU migration to the country, one of the strong arguments used by Brexiteers, as already mentioned. On meeting Merkel, Cameron recalled that he argued that EU migration would be one major factor behind their loss, urging her to help with handling the issue. But Merkel advised that those who changed tack on migration in Germany lost elections. Therefore, Cameron's team decided to reemphasise the economy as one of the major issues in their campaign. To this end, a few days before the referendum, Osborne declared that if Britain left, there should be an emergency budget in order to meet the £30 billion gap in the UK's finance resulting from Brexit. In order to provide this amount of money, Osborne claimed that he should increase income tax, petrol and alcohol duties and inheritance tax and cut spending on health, defence and education.

When the Prime Minister was in his way for a rally in Gibraltar, the British overseas territory next to Spain, to make the case for Remain, a sad event changed his course. At that time, Brexiteers were focusing on migration, which angered Cameron, particularly by seeing Farage standing alongside a poster entitled 'Breaking point'. Indeed, immigration has long been a major concern in the country, as emphasised by Kaufmann (2018) in his *White Shift: Populism, Immigration and the Future of White Majorities*. One of his focal points was the rise of right-wing parties such as UKIP and their anti-immigration attitudes, particularly during the Brexit campaign under Farage's leadership.

The poster was, in Cameron's view, similar to a foghorn to leave the EU. But on hearing about the attack on Jo Cox, Labour MP, he just cancelled the rally and met Fabian Picardo, Gibraltar's Chief Minister, in private. Cox was attacked by a man with a knife and a gun while she was on her way to her constituency in Birstall, West Yorkshire. Cameron, deeply shocked by the event, learned that Cox had died of her injuries, recalling that she was the first MP to be killed since Ian Gow's murder by the IRA (Irish Republic Army) in 1990. More importantly, Cameron was sickened by learning that the attacker had been shouting 'Britain first' or 'This is for Britain,' evidence, according to the Prime Minister, of the relevance of Brexit, bearing the fact that Cox had been a strong Remainer.

Because of Cox's murder, the campaign was stopped for a while, which was Cameron's decision out of respect for an MP he had known well. The Prime Minister joined Corbyn in Batley for a ceremony to remember her, reiterating the words she had articulated in her first speech in the House of Commons in 2015: "We are far more united and have far more in common with each other than things that divide us" (qtd. in Cameron 2019, chap. 46). These words, in Cameron's view, were vital in an age of populism. In other words, Cameron believed that a Labour MP had been insightful in terms of unity of the whole country during the Brexit referendum. Afterwards, Cameron indicated that many experts, along with influential people and countries, argued for Remain, with particular focus on the economy. Some of the people included the head of the NHS, the former heads of the MI5 and MI6,[6] the head of the Church of England and economists such as Stephen Hawking and Tim Berners-Lee. As for countries, they included Britain's allies around the world, notably the US, India, Japan, Australia and Canada.

---

[6] These are the two British intelligence security services. MI5 works at the national level to protect the country from any potential threat whereas MI6 works at the international level for the same purposes.

4. The media, the campaign's final day and Cameron's revelations about the Brexit results

Cameron's account also paid attention to the British media, highlighting his relationship with a number of editors and media owners. He also devoted a chunk of his narrative to the final day of the campaign, along with some revelations about how he lost the battle. The Prime Minister admitted that his team had made mistakes during the campaign, but he claimed that he tried his best to deliver speeches at rallies and fundraising events, in addition to writings to national and local newspapers. He would also express his arguments in debates on Sky News, BBC, ITV, Buzzfeed and Facebook. Yet, Cameron confessed that he was aware of the growing weaknesses in the arguments advanced by Remainers compared to the ones by Leavers, as the campaign was close to an end. This is obviously articulated in the following statement:

> Gradually, every killer argument was being drowned out, and every advantage slowly sunk. Every trait of this age of populism – the prominence of social media, the emergence of fake news, anti-establishment sentiment, growing unease with globalisation, frustration over the level of immigration – appeared to conspire against our cause. It wasn't that Leave was besting us in every battle. It was that the physics of politics seemed to have changed. The upper hand became the losing hand, and the higher ground – which we felt we had captured – was surrounded. (Cameron 2019, chap. 46)

Cameron was particularly concerned with the Eurosceptic press and the way he was infuriated by some owners and editors' strong Euroscepticism. He recalled that the *Daily Mail* foregrounded eighteen stories related to immigration in six weeks, expressing his frustration by such a newspaper, as it had never been an advocate of leaving the EU. Cameron pointed out that Paul Dacre, its editor, was invited for a drink in the Downing Street flat, a few days before Brexit, in the hope of finding an explanation to such an attitude, namely propagating for Leave. Dacre's response was that the newspaper had always been Eurosceptic. Cameron, in turn, replied that he himself had been a Eurosceptic Prime Minister, but this did not systematically mean that he would like to leave the EU.

Cameron emphasised that, although Dacre had not supported his candidacy for the Conservatives' leadership – having been an advocate of Ken Clarke (in December 2005) – both had shown mutual respect. The Prime Minister was hoping to gain Dacre's support by arguing that Brexit would weaken their country's status on the international scene. Such an argument was based on Cameron's awareness that Dacre had been interested in the idea of a European army, given that he had been concerned with Britain's overreliance on the US. Nevertheless, Cameron discovered that Dacre would support Brexit. He therefore turned to Lord Rothermere, the newspaper's owner, inviting him for a coffee in his Downing Street office. Cameron asked Rothermere about Europe and before any response he jokingly said he expected similar views to the Prime Minister's. In contrast, Cameron's guest replied that his views were much stronger than his host's, arguing that Britain's withdrawal would be disastrous. Rothermere added that he may be forced to relocate some of his businesses to some European cities. Therefore, Cameron criticised him for having an editor like Dacre who was campaigning for Brexit. Implicitly, Cameron wished that the *Mail*'s owner would fire Dacre, as had erroneously been reported in the media. Importantly, Cameron highlighted the fact that Dacre would be fired two years after Brexit and replaced by Georgie Greig, a strong Remain advocate.

Apart from losing the *Mail*'s support, Cameron was also worried about the *Sun* and the *Telegraph*, knowing that they would not be supportive. But he gained the support of the *Guardian* and the *Mirror*, two left-leaning newspapers. The *Mirror* has constantly been supporting the Labour party since WWII, implying that Cameron was then in need of such a support irrespective of the newspaper's inclination. This shows that the Brexit campaign gave both the Conservatives and Labour, along with other parties, the opportunity to unite over one common cause, as elaborated in the previous section.

Cameron indicated that his major problem was with the BBC despite its impartiality throughout the campaign. His concern was based on the inability of such an outlet to make the difference between balance and impartiality. Cameron criticised the BBC for giving thousands of businesses supporting Remain equal treatment with just two businesses for Leave, Dyson and JCB.[7] More importantly, the BBC was accused of equating thousands of Remain economists to a tiny number of Brexiteers, giving Economists for Free Trade the same weight as Nobel Prize winners who supported Remainers.

On the final day of the campaign, Cameron recalled that they were on a bus similar to a Noah's Ark, as they would be joined by various people at each visit. Some of the joiners included farmers, veterans, a handbag designer who had just started exporting to the EU, one from Jaguar Land

---

[7] For more details about Dyson see https://www.dyson.co.uk and about JCB see https://www.jcb.com.

Rover and Caroline Lucas from the Green Party. Other ones included a schoolboy, a father, a grandparent and a head teacher after a trip to a school, joined by a midwife and nurses after a trip to Solihull hospital. Their last stop was a rally at Birmingham where they met Brown who delivered an impressive speech. Such a speech, in Cameron's view, was an ideal message on the eve of polling day, presumably reinforcing unity, particularly among the two major parties, namely Labour and the Conservatives.

Nevertheless, Cameron discovered that they had some miscalculations during the campaign, particularly about turnout. He pointed out that his team reckoned that with a 55 per cent turnout, Remainers would have a tight win. Despite a YouGov prediction of a 52-48 win for Remainers, one point higher by ComRes, 53-47, Brexiteers won with a slight margin (52-48). But no one believed that there would be an unexpectedly high turnout, reaching 72.2 per cent. Neither Gibraltar, with 96 per cent of the votes for Remain, nor London and Scotland, for example, were enough to counter the large number of areas which voted Leave. Nancy, Cameron's daughter, told her father that they were losing when results poured in from various areas in the country such as Sunderland, West Oxfordshire, Brentwood, Flintshire, Weymouth and Merthyr Tydfil, all of which voted Leave.

Cameron provided a detailed description of his feelings while waiting for the final results, showing some strength in front of his family members when results were unfolding. He revealed that he had worked on two draft speeches, one for victory and one for defeat, emphasising in the first one the necessity of healing a divided Britain after the Brexit campaign, with particular focus on Britain's rejection of further political integration within the EU project. He recalled that he had some thoughts about reshuffling his cabinet when working on a defeat speech, nominating a few Brexiteers instead of Remainers. But he also thought about his political career, pointing out that he had already informed his inner team that he would leave within a few years irrespective of the result.

Cameron recalled that he accepted defeat after learning that South Buckinghamshire had voted Leave with a 51–49 margin. He then asked everyone in the room to leave him on his own to lie on the sofa looking for some calm, as he would not be able to sleep a wink. Soon after, he learned from his TV that Britain voted Leave, reversing its 1975 decision to be in the European Economic Community (EEC). Cameron, lamenting what he had already shared with his inner team, particularly about staying in power if they lost, decided that he should leave, quoting Lord Carrington on his resignation in 1982 who stated that the British government was facing hard times and that his remaining in power would make it harder.[8] Likewise, Cameron thought that his departure would be inevitable, being aware that his successor's main task would be to secure a Brexit deal through negotiations with Brussels. This would necessitate, in Cameron's view, a new leadership, arguing that, having been a Remain leader, he would have no credibility to deliver on a Brexit deal.

Cameron admitted that such a decision was hard for him on the grounds that he liked neither to surrender nor to see his team lose their jobs. Moreover, he did not like to abandon the plans and policies outlined in their election manifesto which he wished to implement. Yet, his decision was meant to separate his future from the EU issue in public debates. Cameron also confessed that although quitting meant going back on his word, the decision was inevitable after losing the Brexit campaign. He did not like to behave in the same manner as Matteo Renzi, the Italian Prime Minister in the referendum on changing the Italian constitution and the parliamentary system held in the same year as the Brexit referendum, 2016. Renzi had already announced that he would resign had he lost the referendum. Ultimately, he lost with a 20-point margin with a 65 per cent turnout, leading to a victory for anti-establishment and right-wing parties in his country. Cameron believed that had he followed Renzi, by declaring to resign if he lost Brexit, this would have jeopardized the whole campaign, arguing that Renzi's decision had derailed the referendum to the Prime Minister's future rather than the reforms in Italy.

Indeed, Cameron recalled that he had already announced – two days before Brexit – that Britons did not quit. Yet, being fully aware of the reaction of his inner circle, he decided to step down, convinced that Britain would need a new leadership. A conviction shared by people, including his wife Samantha, given that the majority of the Conservatives who had voted Leave would no longer tolerate his premiership. Therefore, after praising Remainers and congratulating Brexiteers, he stated that he would do his best as Prime Minister to lead the country over the next months, adding that he could not steer Britain's ship outside the EU. In other

---

[8] Peter Carington, later Lord Carington, served as Foreign Secretary from 1979 to 1982 under Thatcher. In April 1982, Leopoldo Galtieri, President of Argentina, occupied the Falkland Islands, the British overseas territory next to Argentina, reminiscent of the British Empire. Carington resigned because he could not bear Argentina's seizure of these remote islands, considering it as a humiliating assault. For more details about his resignation see https://www.nytimes.com/1982/04/06/world/foreign-secretary-resigns-britain-falkland-crisis-text-carrington-letter-page-a6.html.

words, he was fully committed to finish his job before the election of a new Prime Minister who would carry out Brexit negotiations with Brussels.

Cameron's account ended up with some family details, particularly showing his children's commitment to the whole campaign and some reactions among their friends. The Prime Minister revealed that Nancy had had a dispute with a school girl while distributing some 'Conservative In' campaign badges to her friends. On being asked whether she was for Leave or Remain, Nancy had responded that she was for Remain. The girl had answered back "Well, f[***] you". Likewise, Nancy had replied: "Well, f[***] you too." Cameron indicated that neither his wife nor he had ever heard their daughter utter the 'f' word before hearing Nancy's story. Such a family detail reveals the level of tension experienced by Cameron's daughter throughout the campaign.

Another story was about Cameron's son Elwen who had been engaged in a school project on the United Nations and human rights. Elwen had been rehearsing with his German classmate playing Angela Merkel, an American one playing Barack Obama, and him playing Cameron. In the aftermath of Brexit, when he was asked whether he would like to carry on with the project, Elwen responded that he would do that for his father. Indeed, Cameron pointed out that Elwen's performance was impressive, causing watching parents to shed tears and staff members to cry. Cameron recalled that, as he had always tried to reassure people, he cracked jokes, but it did not stop his wife from shedding tears as well. Similarly, while subsequently watching a recording of his son's performance, Cameron could not stop his tears, remembering his failure to keep his country in the EU, though showing no regret about his decision to hold the referendum and give people a say on their future in Europe.

Conclusion

The chapter revealed, through a close examination of Cameron's narrative, that the Prime Minister provided a detailed account of the Brexit campaign, offering a better understanding of the whole event. Indeed, it showed that Cameron faced major problems during the Brexit campaign. He was not able to secure support from his two close friends, namely Gove and Johnson. Furthermore, he could not prevent further divisions among his party, though the campaign was an opportunity to unite a large number of politicians on a common ground cause, using their *Stronger In* motto, except for their failure to handle immigration, particularly from the EU. Similarly, Cameron was not able to gain the support of the British media despite his repeated attempts to convince editors and owners of the benefits of remaining in Europe. Equally important, Cameron's reactions to the Brexit results, as well as his family's, offered a new perspective on the whole campaign, mixing up the public and the personal, allowing for a better understanding of the different circumstances shaping such a significant episode in the history of the country. In this sense, the chapter confirmed Coffey's (2014) argument about the significance of autobiographies in unveiling realities about the events as well as their personal lives of the main actors therein, Cameron in particular. The study could therefore be an invitation for further examination of Brexit by opening more avenues and horizons. One possible way to broaden the scope of research on the subject would be by considering more primary sources on Brexit. For example, the current study could be expanded by juxtaposing Cameron's own personal account with those of other figures who played a major role during the campaign such as Farage and Johnson.

References

Cameron, David. 2019. For the Record. London: William Collins. https://fr.z-lib.org.

Coffey, Amanda. 2014. "Analysing Documents." In The Sage Handbook of Qualitative Data Analysis, edited by Flick Uwe, 367-380. London: Sage.

Kaufmann, Eric. 2018. White Shift: Populism, Immigration and the Future of White Majorities. London: Penguin.

Paul, Katheleen. 1997. Whitewashing Britain: Race and Citizenship in the Postwar Era. Ithaca: Cornell University Press, 1997.

CONTRIBUTORS

Nadia ABID is an Assistant Professor of Applied Linguistics the Faculty of Arts and Humanities of Sfax, Tunisia. She is doing research on intercultural language learning and related issues. Her most important articles are: "the Intercultural Speaker across time: A study of Tunisian EFL textbooks" in *Compare: A Journal of comparative and international education 2021,* and "the promotion of the good intercultural speaker through intercultural contacts in a Tunisian EFL textbook" in *Language and Intercultural communication 2020,* 20 (1), 37-49.

Gabriela Andrioai is a Lecturer of English in the Department of Foreign Languages and Literatures, at "Vasile Alecsandri" University of Bacău, Romania. Her main publications are: "Conceptual metaphors of Covid-19 on BBC future: a way of "loading" language with meaning and emotion" (2020) in *Interstudia,*27, 162-171, and "Perceiving Cultural Identity through Comparison, Contrast, Memory and Cognition", 2022 in *Interstudia.* 31, 164-174.

Elena Bonta is a Professor of English in the Department of Foreign Languages and Literatures, at "Vasile Alecsandri" University of Bacău, Romania. Her main publications include: *Understanding language autobiographies, (2015),* LAP LAMBERT Academic Publishing, and "Self- expression in Language Autobiographies. The Language of emotion and its implications for EFL Classes," (2021) which was co-authored with Raluca Galița and published in *Journal of Innovation in Psychology, Education and Didactics* (JIPED), 25 (1), 87-102.

Fathi Bourmeche is an Assistant Professor of Cultural Studies at the University of Sfax, Tunisia. His most important articles include: 1) *Populism and National Identities*, co-edited with Sadok Damak. CONTACT, 2023, and "Ethic Group Experiences with Social Media: The Case of the Cherokee and Native Americans Facebook Group." In *Dismantling Cultural Borders Through Social Media and Digital Communications: How Networked Communities Compromise Identity*, edited by Ngwainmbi, Emmanuel K. Palgrave Macmillan, 2022, pp.331-351.

Elena Ciobanu, PhD, is an Associate Professor of English and American literature at Vasile Alecsandri University in Bacău, Romania. Her main publications include "Interaction as a strategy for creating poetic meaning", in *Perspectives on Interaction, 2013 in* Bonta, E. (ed.), Cambridge: Cambridge Publishing Scholars, 137-148, and "In search of essences: phenomenology and poetics", 2020 in *Romanian Journal of Artistic Creativity*,8(3), New York: Addleton Publishers, 13-28.

Sadok Damak is an Associate Professor of Cultural Studies at the University of Sfax, Tunisia. His latest publications include "*The Nation of Islam's Cautious Return to Americanity in the 2010s: A Cultural Studies Inquiry.* (2020) Newcastle: Cambridge Scholars Publishing, and "Framing Hispanics: The *Los Angeles Times*' Coverage during the 2016 Presidential Electoral Campaign." (2021) in *Shaping Public Opinion*, edited by Fathi Bourmeche and Sadok Damak, 28-55. Sfax, Tunisia: CAEU Med Ali Editions.

Raluca Galiţa is a Senior Lecturer of English in the Department of Romanian language and literature and communication studies, at "Vasile Alecsandri" University of Bacău, Romania. Her main publications include: Galiţa, R. 2022. "Vagueness in hard news. The case of Kabul airport attack, as reported by bbc.com", in *Contemporary Prospects and Tendencies in Language, Literature and Culture.* Selected Proceedings Book, Erzurum, Turcia: Ataturk University Publications, 362-377, Galiţa, R. 2021. "Language in Crisis? An Overview of Textese", in *Cultural Perspectives.* Journal for Literary and British Cultural Studies in Romania, 26, 129-144, and Bonta, E. & R. Galita. 2022. "Online teaching during Covid-19 Pandemic challenges and solutions around the world", in *Studies in Linguistics, Culture and FLT*, "Problems and Solutions in English Studies and FLT", 10 (3), 2022, 66-81.

Asma Moalla is an Assistant Professor of Applied Linguistics at the Faculty of Arts and Humanities of Sfax, Tunisia. Her main publications include: Abid, N. and Moalla, A. (2021). The Intercultural Speaker across time: A study of Tunisian EFL textbooks. *Compare: A Journal of comparative and international education,* and Abid, N and Moalla, A. (2020). The promotion of the good intercultural speaker through intercultural contacts in a Tunisian EFL textbook. *Language and Intercultural communication.* 20 (1), 37-49.

Dorra Moalla is Assistant Professor of Applied Linguistics at the Faculty of Arts and Humanities of Sfax. She teaches grammar, syntax, theoretical linguistics and multimodality. Her main research areas are in visual literacy, multimodality and Functional Linguistics. Her main publications are: Moalla, D. (2018). « Nominal groups in Arabic and English: Experiential Differences and Effect on Tunisian EFL Learners' Translations. In A. Sellami-Baklouti, and Fontaine, L., (Eds.), *Perspectives from Systemic Functional Linguistics*, pp. 288-314. New York: Routledge., and Moalla, D. (2021): The Resemiotisation of Chokri Belaid's talk before his assassination: roles of sign-maker interest and re-reading forces, *Social Semiotics*, DOI: 10.1080/10350330.2021.194924.

Alexandra Moraru is a Teaching Assistant at the Faculty of International Business and Economics within ASE Bucharest. In her research, she is interested in Philology - linguistics, stylistics, discourse analysis. Her main publications include: "Cultural Branding Models in English-Romanian Proverbs -A Conceptual Metaphoric Analysis" 2019, in *Cultural Perspectives* – Journal for Literary Studies in Romania, 24/2019, 27-44, and "Genre Analyisis in Donald Trump's Inauguration Speech", 2017 in *Synergies in Communication*, 16-17 November 2017, ASE Bucharest, the 6th International Conference, electronic version 206- 212.

INDEX